When I Return...

Letters from a World War II soldier to his sweetheart on his journey from Baltimore to the Pacific and back

Written by Allen H. Nauss

Transcribed and edited by his daughter
Christine N. Simmons

Published by Christine N. Simmons
Laurel, Maryland

ISBN-13: 978-1727740707
ISBN-10: 1274070X

Acknowledgements

This book has been "in the works" for many years. Above all, I would like to thank my late mother for her habit of saving just about everything, including my father's letters. It spurred me into the challenge of compiling this book.

I would like to give thanks to those friends whom I relied on for input during the various steps of putting this book together, especially to Bridget Blake, Diane and Jeff Nesmeyer, Vicki Hutchins, and Chip Pettebone for their recommendations. I am deeply indebted to Ann and James Tanner for graciously offering their professional expertise and guidance in the book publishing process during the book's development and I am grateful for Beth Bandy's help with helping to exhibit the photographs at their best. I am especially grateful for the continued loving encouragement and endless patience by Dennis Green in my pursuit of the publication of this book.

For Dad, in loving memory

Allen Howard Nauss

Foreword

Like many other researchers, I was told that the service records for my father, Allen Howard Nauss, were "lost" in the St. Louis archives fire. A number of years later, I made a second bid to obtain his records. This book is my attempt to reconstruct his military service through his letters and available portions of his service record. Great moments in history are how we can learn from our past, but there is also great value in learning the stories of "the everyday man" living through historic times. My father was not in combat, on the front lines, was not an officer, and did not help develop battle strategies. He was one of the many necessary, but often unsung, support personnel who served during the war. After my mother, Mercia "Mer" Stabler Nauss, died, I discovered a trove of letters that my father had sent to her during his extremely varied World War II military service. I have only one letter that she wrote back to him.

My father was a quiet man who enjoyed puttering around the house and was very good at "jury-rigging" various fixes. He was calm and private, never talking about his wartime experiences to me. As with a popular television commercial, "When E.F. Hutton talks, people listen", when my father offered an opinion, it was worth listening to. Not a passionate man, at least in front of my brother and me, I never saw my parents exchange more than a peck on the cheek. My mother had a tendency to get frustrated when trying to explain things to us and she would tell us to go ask our father for explanations. A patient teacher, his explanations usually made perfect sense. My mother was the worrier in our family and my father would often say that he didn't need to worry…that she worried enough for both of them.

In reading my father's letters, I was somehow surprised to discover the passionate side of him, a person who could write to his "Dearest Vixen", "Dearest Mer" or "Hi Darling" on an almost daily basis, often writing five to eight-page letters. His signoffs included "All my love", "Forever Yours", "Your Man", and "Allen", followed by his own signoff, a capital A and N linked together with a horizontal line through the middle.

Through his letters I came to know my father as an optimistic and usually patient man who dealt with government bureaucracy, rampant rumors that abounded about furloughs and service discharges, who had patience with non-native speakers, came up with creative fixes for their budding photography business, and who had the ability of adding comfort to his sometimes austere surroundings.

Although my father received training in a number of different specialty areas, his position on Saipan was as the supervisor of a truck tire shop manned by Korean workers conscripted by the Japanese and who were anticipating the war's end so that they could return home. It was interesting to note that although he used a slang term for them, he always capitalized the word as "Gooks" in his letters. Along with the inclusion of weighty subjects such as why he wouldn't marry the love of his life right away are his interesting tales of day-to-day living arrangements and dealings with the military.

Allen graduated from high school in Baltimore, MD. He then had two years of ROTC training while at the University of Maryland. He transferred to the University of Baltimore's night law program while working during the day. He did his basic training in North Carolina at the Seymour Johnson Air Force base. Subsequently, he was stationed at Fort Myer in VA and was believed to have been an MP at the Pentagon. He was stationed in the Army at Lake Charles, LA, Camp Houge, TX, Fort Maxey, TX, and Camp Bowie, TX. He received chemical weapons training at Rocky Mountain Arsenal, CO, returned to Camp Bowie, TX and then departed from Fort Lawton, WA for Saipan. He received his discharge from the Army at Fort George G. Meade, MD in 1946. He married his sweetheart and subsequently received a law degree from the University of Maryland.

Throughout this book, some names are listed only as first or last names. In a limited number of cases, I know their full names. Sometimes only a first or last name only was known.

When I Return...

Table of Contents

WHEN I RETURN....

CHAPTER 1
Starting the Journey

Undated, Christmas Card from Allen, U.S. Army Air Forces, Seymour Johnson Field, N. Car.

Undated postcard, from the Court of Two Sisters, New Orleans [sketch with *The Romantic Rendezvous for lovers of the Famous New Orleans Creole and French Dishes in the Vieux Carre's Largest and most Beautiful Patio*]
Got here at 11:00 PM and as first train to Lake Charles is 8:00 PM I've been snooping around the Old French Quarter. Saw this bit of fluff and thought of you. Hope it will wipe away a tear from my departure.

Tues., 11.28.1944, Base Ordnance Office, USAAF, Lake Charles, LA [Along with a letter enclosed from Rev. Arrowsmith, Canon at The Pro-Cathedral Episcopal Church in Baltimore, Md. congratulating them on their engagement and commenting that he thought it was a good idea to postpone getting married until after the war. Also, a letter back to Rev. Arrowsmith that Allen doubted that Mercia had told Rev. Arrowsmith that she hoped he would marry her at The Pro-Cathedral.]

Did I make a *faux pas* by addressing him as "Dear Canon Arrowsmith"? And I addressed the envelope as "Rev. H.N. Arrowsmith, Canon".

Well, we are in another barracks now and leave it to little Allen to snag the only single bunk (not double deck) in the place. This place is about a block further from the mess hall but it's as close as possible to where we work. It isn't 50 yards from where we sleep at night to where we work. We can sleep to 7:59 and still be at work by 8:00. Breakfast is only served 'til 7:15. I don't like to skip breakfast so this morning I got up, ate breakfast and then went back to bed 'til almost 8:00.

There are a lot more attractive ways I could have your two photos framed other than sealed between two sheets of Plexiglas. However, that way it is small, light, flexible, dustproof, moisture proof, etc., and can and will be with me even if I end up in the wettest, dirtiest foxhole ever dug.

I'm surprised you seem to get so much satisfaction that I am still stateside. I think most girls would rather feel their betrothed was getting a little glory and fighting for his "Nell" [or whomever] instead of still being stateside training and equipping other Joes to do the fighting.

Sun., 12.3.1944, no location given
Hank Hatter seems to be in Africa watching for subs in the Atlantic. He says he hopes I won't get married 'til we can go on a good stag drunk at home (Hank sure has changed) with the old crowd. He says that he has lost contact with most of his girls and will have to get some new ones on the string after the war.

Mother says Bud still called and seemed very disappointed about washing out. She also said Charles Rausch had called for my address. He has just returned from Italy and has just seen his four-month old son. He had two planes shot out from under them and two of his crew are missing and three are in the hospital but he is OK. I know it's no way to talk, but whenever I hear "God takes care of fools & drunkards," I always think of Rausch as the fool and Bud as the drunkard, and both have lots of luck.

[His mother wrote to him about meeting Mer's "clan" and he told Mer not to be afraid of his mom, "she won't bite you".]

Mon., 12.11.1944, Co. D, 75th I.A.T.B., Camp Maxey, Tex.- Letter to Allen from Mer, returned as NO RECORD, IARTC [Infantry Army Replacement Training Center] Camp Maxey, Tex.

Thurs., 12.14.1944, U.S. Army letterhead
I bet by now you feel like a charter member of the "engaged girls with men scattered all over the world and waiting for letters, furloughs, and the war". I'll bet you're even used to wearing the same ring on the same finger all the time and I pray that not much more time will pass until you have to get used to wearing two rings on that finger.

Call me cold or what you will, but I could never see the point of saving old letters. However, I do have three of yours now. I learned my lesson when I moved to Maxey that I should keep one or two so I can read and re-read them until I get mail.

At this writing, I still don't know your reaction to the Canon Arrowsmith's letter. Remember he said, "Best wishes for my service in the Air Corps."? Next time you see him you might ask him if that goes for the infantry too. I also wonder what your reaction will be to yours truly being an infantry *doggie*.

Don't get the idea that I or anyone else likes this place any better than I do, but I'll point out some of the good things. You know how it is; any picture is just as light or as dark as you paint it. The place has five movies so you have a choice of pictures instead on like L.C. [Lake Charles] where there were only two and each showed the same film. Then too, this used to be a big camp but it's almost a ghost town now and there are no waiting lines for shows. There is plenty of mud, but we've been here five days now and it hasn't rained yet. We use china plates at mess instead of metal trays (first I've hit since Fort Myer). The food is better than L.C. or Maxey. I do miss the trees 'tho. I think it's high time we had some sort of lease lend to move some of the extra trees from up north down here.

This training is rough and tiring but in some ways it is sort of fun. We spent part of this afternoon crowding down in foxholes and letting a tank roll over us, just to get used to it and to prove to the doubtful ones that if you dig deep enough a tank will pass over and not hurt you.

You know it's strange, but ever since I took ROTC at University of Maryland I've sort of had an idea I'd make a good infantry soldier and it looks like maybe I'll get a chance to prove it. When I first went into the Army, I thought they were goofy for not sticking me into the infantry right away since I had had two years of infantry ROTC. Now I've ended up in the infantry to make my fifth branch of the service in two yrs. If I could get into the Navy now I could write a book on "Life in the Armed Forces". One funny thing is that when we finish this training we get the classification of "Infantry Rifleman" and that is just what we got when we finished basic training at Fort Myer and it is still on my service record.

Mon., 12.18.1944, written on back of a letter from his friend, Bud
I am rushed for time as it's late now, there are rifles to clean, packs to make up, etc., and we are leaving for the range early in the morning.

I just got this today and the quickest way to tell you is to pass it on. Keep it under your hat 'til Christmas, but I think it's OK to tell you as you are part of me.

Don't mind the fact that he only mentions surprise about us 'cause I know Bud and I know he is pleased and you can well see he has plenty on his mind!

I think Bud made a swell choice and I was cheering for Jane. I know you will like her.

Mon., 12.25.1944, Austin, Tex., U.S. Army letterhead [Christmas]
Believe it or not, the pipe cleaners were the first gift I used. I was in Dallas and while I unwrapped my things, I was smoking my pipe and wishing I had bought one or two pipe cleaners in my limited baggage.

I bet when you sat down at a table with another girl in a crowded tearoom you never would have dreamed that your soldier friend would be your fiancé and would be having a Christmas Eve date with that girl in Texas. I planned to go to Dallas this weekend with no idea that Jo lived there. Then you mentioned that I might want the camera in case I got to Dallas and looked up Jo. So I decided while I was in Dallas I would try to locate Jo (without address). Three of us left here and got to Dallas (65 mi.) by bus only, no train. The first thing we did was to go to the U.S.O. and learn we could stay at a private home or YWCA. We took the Y because of its central location. Beds good, good big free breakfast served 'til 11:30 AM both mornings and everyone at the U.S.O. and Y seemed to go out of his and her way to take care of us and nothing was too good for us. I'll bet at least 500 servicemen stayed at the YW the weekend! We had only two complaints: the mirrors were too low for men and the pool was closed. Then, after we had a place to sleep, I grabbed a phone book and looked up "Cox, Jo". I thought there would be about two dozen and I could call them all. There are at least 300 Cox names listed in Dallas! Then I called Girl Scout Headquarters-closed. I talked to several women in the YW and finally found one who knew an official of the Girl Scouts and she said she would call this other woman in the A.M. (about 10:30 PM then). Then I went out with the boys, saw Dallas, and got a load of Christmas spirit. Then around 2 AM, I had an idea. The city directory! And there it was. All I had to do was find a crisscross phone book and get the phone number. So Sunday morning after breakfast I called and 'sho nuft there was Jo. She asked me out for Christmas dinner which they were having Sun. 1:00 PM. The weather was a light rain or mist. You could not get a cab for love or money. (I only tried money). We had dinner with three other couples and I bet that turkey weighed a good 17 lbs. Turkey, smashed sweet potatoes, beets, stuffing, broccoli, cranberry sauce, olives, salad, and lots and lots of things including homemade rolls, fruitcake, cookies., etc. Then Jo and I took the car and went to call on some friends of hers and tour their new house. We returned home and played cards for about an hour. Then Jo changed so we could go dancing. Taylor could be proud of how she looked. Wearing her hair down (I like it better than up), with a black velvet dress, fur coat and fur hat. I love those fur hats that sort of look like Dan'l Boone and I don't think I've ever seen any women that didn't look good in one. We had to drink beer as both of us are still used to Baltimore and not in the habit of carrying a bottle. No mixed drinks are sold in Dallas and everyone must carry a bottle around and then buy ice and soda, etc. We had plenty to talk about and it was good to be able to mention B'dere [Belvedere Hotel], Peabody Bookshop, etc. and not get a blank stare! We left about 12:30 AM and it was raining hard. I wanted to take Jo home but she wouldn't let me and insisted on dropping me off at the YW and driving home alone.

Sun., 1.28.1945, on U.S. Army stationary, location unknown

Don't mind me if I kid you, but that is just one of the things I love about you- I never know what the hell is coming next! The answer is no. Just plain NO. Now I do expect to stay stateside a little longer but the answer is still no. I know the arguments for it- "We should grab what pleasure from life that we can now.", "It wouldn't cost any more to live than it costs us now", and "We'd get the extra money of an allotment", etc., etc. It is still no. Here is why: As long as I am in the Army and even more as long as I am in the infantry, there is a very good chance, in fact it is almost certain that I will get into combat before the war ends. Now, my training and luck are as good if not better than the next

Joe's, but there is always the chance I won't come back. That alone would be rough for a girl, but then there is always the prospect of a child. Between us, we could name almost a dozen girls with children whose fathers are missing. That's not only unfair to the girl, but unfair to a child who had no choice in the matter yet who would suffer the most. Sure, I want to marry you and maybe I will decide any day now to marry you anyway, but I hope we will both be strong enough to put it off.

Now for the news. My orders read I am to proceed to Camp Bowie, Tex. on or about 30 Nov. 1945. I guess I am going as an armorer as about 15 of us are on the shipment and about seven listed on the order as armorers. We don't know if it is jungle training, cadre, or what the deal is, except that Camp Bowie is not a P.O.E. [Port of Embarkation] so it looks like I may be stateside for a little while longer. Don't expect too good a deal out of this Bowie action. For all I know they are making up an outfit down there that is all set to go. I can't find a soul who knows a thing about Bowie-where the camp is, how large, near where, what sort of outfit, etc. The opinions seem to show it is about 300-400 miles south of here and around 60-90 miles from San Antonio. At least it might be warmer there and I hope not so much mud.

In addition to your very, very sweet letter today, (Wanna get married?) I had one from "long lost Sherman". (Tell people you are going overseas with the infantry and even Sherman writes you a letter!) He is still at Wright Field, Dayton, OH and now has Betty with him. Betty's mother sent her a clipping of the engagement of a friend of Betty's and the groom turned out to be Bud! Andy says he was home for Christmas and saw ____ Martin and his new wife. (Seems everybody has one-must try it sometime.)

Well, the gang got away OK Friday and I hope you got my wire. It was a regular circus getting that mob underway. They stocked up for a long train ride with plenty of food, liquor, and reading matter. No liquor allowed on troop trains but… Well, they fell out at 2:00 PM and could not carry handbags. All they could carry was a kit of toilet articles and everything else had to go into a barracks bag, which would be in the baggage car for the whole trip. They fell back into the barrack to get rid of the stuff. They had oranges, apples, loaves of bread, cheese, crackers, cakes, canned fruit salad, jars of olives, etc. They filled pockets with cans, jars, etc. put loaves of bread inside our shirts and every damn thing! You would have died laughing! Fellows shipping were selling liquor to fellows staying for half of what it cost them. One screwball had two quarts and decided to drink it all in the half hour they had. When time came to leave, he was as limp and cold as a dead fish and out like a light. They had to lift him into a car and take him to the train! However, I don't think there was a liquor check and those who tried it got it aboard OK. They did pretty well by having only four or five AWOL's when it was train time. One fellow in our barrack had won about $300.00 in card and crap games and paid $125.00 to hire a car to take him to Denver. He told us he was going and everyone just watched him pack, say goodbye and take off. That's the first guy most of us have ever seen who said he was going "over the hill" who really did. Ones who go over usually are ones who don't say a word, but just go to town and don't come back. Damn fools, every last one of them.

Nobody likes to ship with a lot of dirty clothes, so now every time I shower and change I also wash the things I just took off. I'll whip an airmail out to you as soon as I learn my address at Bowie (just like the racetrack). By the way, your airmails make it here in two days, but from the sound of things, mine don't reach you nearly that fast.

Fri. another Joe and I toasted the departure of our friends with a large steak in town. I wish you could have been there. They brought me one side of the steer and him the other side. It was the largest steak I have ever seen since pre-war Black Bottle and good too.

I had hoped maybe headquarters would get all crossed up and give me a delay en route on my shipment to Camp Bowie (Maxey, Houge, Bowie-just say that aloud!)

The little bell [believed to be a gift from his best friend Bud], now with my dog tags, has been silenced by a piece of leather curled inside the bell and around the clapper.

You speak of the choice of my going to Meade and over in the infantry or my going as armorer. Even if I do go as an armorer I will still be in the infantry and I will be an infantryman plus an armorer.

CHAPTER 2
Camp Bowie, Brownwood, Texas

Wed.,2.7.1945, U.S. Army letterhead, Camp Bowie, Brownwood, Tex.
Gad! I have so much to say and so much to answer that I don't know where to start. I'm sort of confused anyway. For the past half hour, I've been trying to figure out your code system. My mind isn't as alert as it used to be and it never was so hot. The main trouble turned out to be that your list of phrases got mixed up with another of your letters when I opened two of them at once. The code idea is good. Very good. A lot better than mine and even 'tho the phrases are about things dear to both of us, I doubt if I could learn all of those word for word. So, may I submit a change? I will return the list of phrases and you can discard it. Then, you write a nice sweet note to me in longhand and on a note folder about the size of this phrase list

Dear Allen,
(26 sweet, connected sentences)
As always,
Mer

Well, at least I have started to get your mail coming straight to Bowie. So now, we will be back to normal for a while. Okay, I will start to reverse my letters and send most of them to your office and once and awhile one to "331". I think one of your letters just set a record! It was postmarked Feb. 5, at 4 PM and I got it Feb. 6 at 5 PM. Only 25 hours form your hands to mine. And almost as though to prove that won't always happen-the letter I got today (Feb. 7) was mailed 7:30 PM Feb. 3). Both letters were mailed directly to Bowie and both have#13 on the postmark so I guess they were mailed near your home instead of from the office.

The purpose of a Q.M. Trk. Co. like this is to drive truck convoys. You know- Burma Road, etc. This unit is just training now and will be for quite a while. In camp, the armorers will make repairs on weapons, etc. On convoy, there will be about 50 trucks with a driver and asst. driver on each. Interspaced in the convoy will be four half-track scout cars. Each scout car has a cal. 50 machine gun and a gunner (the armorers). So that's the deal-machine gunner to keep planes, etc. away from the convoy. In case you don't know: a half-track is an armored car with wheels in front and a rack like a tank instead of rear wheels. I like the sound of that business.

As for now, I am still teaching classes and I just remembered that I forgot to hand in a lesson plan for my two-hour class on carbines tomorrow.

Uniforms? I wasn't down to only one uniform- it was two, but they were both O.D. [olive drab] uniforms. Today I got all my stuff so all is Jake now and I will have to stick around the barrack in coveralls 'til Sat. as I put my O.D.'s in the cleaners this evening. Now I have to have my hat braid changed and put on the buff-colored Q.M. braid. About the best thing I liked about the infantry was the blue braid that matched my blue eyes. (I love me and you- who do you love?)

Soon people will think you are a regular camera bug carrying the camera around, going to fires, etc. More fun.

I have flunked one or two things in my time, but I never flunked anything except gym! Maybe instead of trying to beat my time, your friend should get you to coach him (in studies).

I've heard quite a bit about San Antone and would like to get there sometime. All the Texans seem to call it "San Antone" instead of San Antonio.

You know, I think you have got a bit of the jitters. Stop worrying about the cooking and housekeeping! We'll get along fine and have lots of fun.

All in all this setup isn't so bad. I have to wear another shoulder patch now. My uniforms and hats have almost worn out from this constant changing of patches and braid. Maybe I will be assigned to a WAC [Women's Army Corps] outfit someday! The current patch is for the 4th Army. It is a red square on edge with a white four-leaf clover. Still am not sure if I will stay with this outfit, but it is beyond all doubt that as an outfit they will be here for at least three months. (By "here", I mean "stateside".)

Am I sorry I was so impulsive in Oct.? That proves you have a touch of jitters! Snap out of it! I love you more every day and I still think putting a claim on you was the best thing I have ever done. What's more, it wasn't impulsive! I had planned that for weeks before I got my furlough even if I couldn't remember the words I was going to prepare.

Wonder if I should send the bell back to Bud or hold on to it awhile and see what is cooking? Maybe if Bud is flying, even 'tho it's only on training flights, he may have more use for its luck than I right now.

Mon., 2.19.1945, Camp Bowie, Brownwood, Tex.
We just heard over the radio that starting Mon. nightclubs, etc. would close promptly at midnight. My first thought was that if the restriction is still in effect the next time I get home you still would not get home any earlier from our dates.

Darling, I think you should take your ring to be engraved. If we put it off it may still not have been engraved years after we have been married and may always be something we just put off. I don't think anything would do except "Vix to Vixen". It may be unusual, but we are unusual people. It may not be conventional, but "conventions be damned."

The other day you mentioned getting a carton of cigarettes. When I heard that, I already had a carton for you in my footlocker. I was trying to figure out how to wrap it since fellows say that if it looks like cigarettes it often vanishes in the mail these days. Now you will have a surplus of weeds, but you always have friends, so you won't have trouble getting rid of them.

Still need a lot more spare time if I am ever to finish "The Robe". In my opinion, most persons would get more out of reading that book and really thinking about it, than attending church for a solid year.

Sat. 2.24.1945 [Post card from Fort Worth, Tex.
I managed to work a deal so that I could leave Bowie in AM and got here at Sat. noon. Nice town and most civilians I've seen for a long time.

Sun., 2.25.1945, Camp Bowie Tex. (Fort Worth letterhead with picture of cityscape and "*For 'whoopee' and mirth…there's no 'whoopee' like the "whoopee" at Fort Worth".'*)

Thought of going to church this morning but since I two-timed you last night it will do me better to write to you. They had a dance here last night at the service center and I weakened and played wolf for the first time since I left you. Even as bad as I was, I was not very bad. I only danced with one girl and I explained to her that I was engaged to a wonderful, blond, charmer in Md. and I wanted to dance 'cause the music and floor were good and there was nothing else to do. She was the best-looking blonde on the floor. (You know I always go for only the best) but she still could not come anywhere near you.

There are no USOs in Fort Worth. Instead, the people of Fort Worth run this huge "service center". It was formerly a dept. store and in size and location like Stewart & Co. Two floors are for ballroom, lounge, 'phones, games, etc. and the other three floors for dorms. It's the largest service center in the country and very well run.

Fri. evening I was detailed for guard duty for the first time since I have been at Bowie. They use the old Army system of "bucking for orderly", i.e. the most polished man of the guard is relieved from duty and the next AM he reports to the Col. as his orderly. Then the Col. usually tells him there is nothing to do and he just lays around the barrack and sleeps. Needless to say, yours truly made orderly since few soldiers shine brass, etc. like we had to do in M.P. and cadets. So I didn't have any guard duty and then Sat. AM the Col. must have been feeling good or liked my looks 'cause he asked me if I'd like a pass. I was able to leave for Fort Worth Sat morning while the rest of the camp couldn't leave 'til 5 PM. This would be a wonderful town and day if you were only here with me, but as it is, I will go back early since it's raining and transportation will be crowded.

Mon., 2.26.1945, Camp Bowie, Tex. letterhead, addressed to Mercia c/o her work address)
These coming days with you are going to be not only Bud's wedding, but also our Christmas together, our New Years together, my Birthday together. Just plain days together. I guess it will have to be our Easter together too because if I make it in time for the wedding I will have to leave before Easter. It will be the first Easter that I didn't get home won't it? I just finished a letter to Bob and Emily that I started last Tuesday. I guess they think I am in Germany by now.

OK, so your eyes are blue- but should I know? I am in love. Do you think the dog we should get should be an English Sheep Dog- so one of the males in the family could have a lot of hair?

We**d., 2.28.1945**, Camp Bowie, Brownwood, Tex.
Bud had better not change his wedding date now. If I start trying to shift furlough dates around again after all the fuss I've made; someone will crawl my frame. If the date were set back a few days and I could get the furlough three or four days later, I could be home for Easter. As it is, I will wait and meanwhile figure on the 17th.

When I'm home –we'll have to get hold of some horses. *N'est-u-pas?*

I don't seem to know Elaine. Lawd, yes, you will find Geo. [his brother] has former girlfriends everywhere you go. You will find people know what you're talking about if you refer to me as "George Nauss's brother". I would not say he's bashful, but he has a sort of quiet, shy line that girls seem to go for. We like to go our own ways and have only had about three or four double dates and then only because we both wanted the car and were going to the same dance or something like that. We almost never talk of our dates and there are only a very few girls that both of us have dated.

Last night we had a night convoy problem and drove 60 miles with 20 trucks. We were out 'til 1:00 AM and everyone was pretty well beat except a few of us. Four of us who were gunners etc. didn't have to drive; so we wrapped up in our overcoats and bedded down with two large comforters on the floor of a closed truck and slept thru the whole convoy.

Wed. 2.28.1945, Camp Bowie, Brownwood, Tex.
I just finished writing you and mailed the letter but I was still here at the service club and did such a damn fool trick that I have to tell you about it. Remember that little white skull charm that I used to wear with my dog tags? We got those at our Jr. Tea Dance at F.P.H.S. [Forest Park High School] and I kept it on the lapel of my sports coat and then later with my dog tags. One evening at Seymour Johnson I was polishing my dog tags and left the liquid jewelers rag on the tags to make it dry faster. The skull whet up in a puff of smoke. I was smoking my pipe when I mailed your letter a few minutes ago and I proceeded to tamp down the ashes with the end of my pen as I've done hundreds of times before. I use, or should say used-I don't know what you would call it. It's the end that doesn't have the cap over it. At any rate, there was a puff of smoke and now the end of my pen is burnt off and my pipe smells like I have been smoking movie film. I do the damnest things!

Glad to hear that Nickie is home so you should have plenty of company. You mention Nickie and Lee as tied for your second-best girlfriend. Whom do you consider your best?

Please don't worry your head of blond curls about the curfew. It won't kill us to get home at a reasonable hour and we can always start out a little earlier. Remember, you said I could have one night per week with the boys? If Bud does get married the 17th and it is possible to get Bill Myer, we really should give Bud a stag party the night before he is married. I know Bud has counted on that for a number of years and it would mean a lot to him. I think that should be done if possible even if it means taking my first night home.

Been doing a lot of truck convoys lately, but my machine guns aren't needed, so aren't mounted. Convoys need to be patrolled by a motorcycle to keep trucks closed up- so Nauss used to be an M.P and the machine guns aren't needed just now- so it looks like I talked myself into another job. You would laugh your head off if you could only see me tearing up and down and in and out of the line of trucks astride "the Iron Rabbit" My only trouble is that one Lt. likes to ride also and he takes my job over about half of the time. It sure is fun 'tho!

Tues, 3.6.1945, Camp Bowie, Brownwood, Tex.
I did not think I would be able to write you tonight as Tuesday is our night for "convoy night problems". Today we had a big review and inspection by Maj. Gen. Lucas, the commanding general of the 4th Army. Tomorrow I am teaching another machine gun class and since the general is still here in the area and may take a look at the class the Lt. asked me to stay in tonight and prepare things for the class so it will go off without a hitch. I felt like telling him that my classes usually do go off without a hitch and that there was nothing to prepare. But why should I open my big mouth when I could write to you instead of riding around in a truck 'til 1:00 AM?

Well, here's one and hold your hat 'cause it's rough on both of us. Yes, it is the furlough. Fourth Army inspectors will test our outfit from the 15th to 19th and furloughs are to be frozen 'til about the 20th so everyone will be here. It isn't as bad as it could be because I'll still get my furlough, but unless I can do some fancy talking, I won't get home 'til around the 24th or 25th at best and will miss Bud's wedding, but coming home to you and we'll still have that 'tho it won't be as soon as we had hoped.

I wish the Lt. would quit walking in and stopping to talk. I am about the only man not out on the problem and I am sitting here in the day room with a raft of open machine-gun manuals and writing this. Most of the others are around because they are goofing off from the problem too and they realize I don't have to study up just to tell a class how to disassemble and assemble a gun, but it is a good idea to look like you have good intentions.

Being in Washington and at the Pentagon spoiled me for being impressed by rank and brass. We got so used to seeing stars and brass that now it leaves me cold and everyone else seems to be all hopped up as soon as they hear the word "general".

I like the idea of your having time off from the office so we can have more time together, but you can see that you had better wait 'til I get there before you make any real arrangements for a substitute. I think you know that your meeting me at the train would mean as much to me as it would to you, but the day and hour of my departure from here are so vague and then the travel time takes from 40-50 hrs. depending on the connections, etc. so the best idea would be still to let me come to you. If it does look like I'll arrive at a sane hour I'll wire you en route if I have a chance and you may be able to meet me after all or at least know when to expect me but please don't count on being able to meet me at the train.

I learned Bud's wedding was to be formal when my father wrote that he would have to dig out his tux and see if he could still get into it. I don't think much of the formal idea myself, but if Bud & Jane want it that way, well OK.

Remember darling that I love you more than anyone or anything on earth and that even 'tho they can keep us apart for a little while longer now sooner or later we will be together again. Will keep you posted on my plans, schemes, setbacks, failures and hopes.

Fri., 3.9.1945, Camp Bowie, Brownwood, Tex.
I am so tired I may fall asleep before I finish. However, I must explain the letter I wrote and the wire I sent today. Wednesday and Thursday the Capt. wasn't in a good mood so I steered clear of him. This morning I found him feeling good, so I cried on his shoulder-got him to agree to let me go on Tues. the 13th when the 4th Army physical training test is over. This inspection test will take from the 13-16 but the 13th is the physical fitness tests and as the company must qualify so many men and I am one of the few who are of sound mind and limb, the Capt. wants me to be here for at least that. The main thing is I will be home and in time for the wedding. Will call you as soon as I hit town. I understand there is to be a dry run of the wedding Fri. evening and then a buffet supper. I expect you to go with me. There won't be anything for you to do at the dry run except meet people, but "Where I go thou will go." I expect to be home about 10 days and I don't want you more than arm's length any more than need be.

Must get back to the barrack and hit the sack as we are going out on the range early in the morning and I'll have to keep the boys from shooting each other.

Sun., 3.11.1945, Camp Bowie, Brownwood, Tex.
I can't go into town because my blouse is in the cleaners. I keep looking at timetables, making a list of things to remember to pack, etc. If it weren't for getting my blouse and overcoat from the cleaners tomorrow, I could leave on a moment's notice and here I have until Tuesday evening to sweat out.

Bill Wilson refers to the wedding as the "Big Parade" and it sounds like one! 300 at the church, 150 at reception, and seven ushers, etc., etc. One thing about this wedding business-we will get a chance to see many people we've missed before, Bill Meyer, Greenwalts, etc. I will enclose Bud's latest letter, as there isn't time to answer it.

I'll have to stick around here Tuesday 'til the physical fitness test is over and I hope it'll be over by noon. It doesn't make much difference as long as I leave by 6:00 PM to get the 11:30 PM Santa Fe out of Fort Worth for Chicago. The only trains out of Brownwood are 9:30 AM and 12:50 AM so the best thing is to use a bus or hire a car to get to Ft. Worth.

[Letter from Bud: Bill will step aside if Allen can come home and Allen will be best man. Ushers include Bill Wilson, Bill Meyer, John Archer, Jack Henderson, Don Greenwalt, Henry Moran, and Ned Ordt if he comes home. He expects to go to Ellington from Houston for nine weeks next month.]

Mon., 3.12.1945, [Western Union telegram]
Disregard letter. Will arrive Baltimore between Thursday midnight and Friday noon. Allen

Wed., 3.14.1945, Western Union telegram [c/o Mer's office]
Will arrive Penn Station 4:10 PM Thursday. Lots of love. Allen

Wed., 3.21.1945, Camp Bowie, Tex. [addressed to her home]
We have rain again today. This makes the third straight day and now Texas has too much mud for man or beast.

We had a big 4th Army inspection yesterday and it took up the whole day. They checked over our machine guns, rifles, and carbines but we weren't gigged too badly.

If, in your travels, you happen to see anything that would make a good wedding or birthday gift for Bud, please call my mother. Bud's birthday is Mar. 15 and I have asked my mother to get both gifts, but could not suggest a thing and doubt if she has any idea what to get.

Fri., 3.30.1945, Postcard, Texarkana, Arkansas/Texas
"Here we sit like birds in the wilderness." We have been sitting on this _ _ _ _ train in the station for 10 hours now and it has not moved an inch!

Fri., 3.30.1945, Red Cross Canteen, Texarkana, Arkansas/Texas
I just wrote you an hour and a half ago, but here I am again. I took your letter upstairs to the station, mailed it, washed, shaved, brushed my teeth, clipped my fingernails and even shined my brass. Then I went into the canteen and had coffee and sandwiches. They are having more steady business at that canteen today than they have had for a long time. Even the trainmen don't know if we will be stranded a few more minutes or a few days. They told us we could go up to the station and wait as they announce up there before either train moves; but most of us just go up to send wires, wash and eat. It is more comfortable to wait on the train and not crowded so most of us can sit with our feet propped up on the seat opposite.

Still have the *Readers Digest* to cover and plenty of people to talk to who are in the same boat or train. (Maybe we could get there easier if this was a boat.)
You can tell Jo that Tex.as is a wonderful place.... for Texans. I was stranded here once before, on my way from Lake Charles to Camp Maxey. Address all future letters to the Texas & Pacific RR, Coach #1360, Texarkansas Station, Tex.-Ark. The train is rumored to be going to Fort Worth first then back to Dallas.

2 PM: Well, we have been sitting on the train in the station, not moving, for 10 hours. I just walked up to the canteen and got another coffee and sandwich-not that I wanted it so much, but it was something to do.
4 PM: Still here. Food and water are holding out well.
5:20 PM: We moved! Trainman says we are heading for Fort Worth and hope to reach there about 3:00 AM.
5:45 PM: Stopped again. Hope it's short.

8:50 PM: Going along fairly steady now and I guess we will make Fort Worth by 3:00 AM. We are going a roundabout way and thru Paris, which is the way, we went to get to Maxey.
2:10 AM: Pulling into Fort Worth sooner than we expected. Will mail this and be on my way again. Only four-hour trip from here to Bowie.

Mon., 4.2.1945, U.S. Army, Camp Bowie, Brownwood, Tex.
I've long been aware of your many accomplishments, but until now, I did not know that poison pen letters were among them. I pay tribute to that masterpiece of nasty communications you whipped up for my benefit.
However, if I may be so bold as to comment; I would like to point out that the last three lines spoiled the wonderful effect built up in the body of the letter.

As you no doubt know by now my washing out was the cause of your not receiving the courtesies you expect.
My first reaction to note was: "Lord! After all I've been thru I was supposed to be writing thank-you notes."
I'll enclose the little masterpiece as you may enjoy rereading it some dark rainy night after you've beaten some poor grandmother with her own crutches.
[Signed Pfc. Nauss, A.H.
P.S. You better dash off a line and say you're sorry. Love Allen
P.P.S. New Address:

Pfc. Allen H. Nauss 33384264
93rd Academic Sqdn.
TS AAFTC
Yale Univ., New Haven, Conn.

P.P.P.S. Daniel and I just started rooming together today and now we're going out, mail this, and get dead drunk.

Tues., 4.3.1945, U.S. Army, Camp Bowie, Brownwood, Tex.
They got rid of the "Iron Rabbit" so maybe I won't break my neck after all.

Found out that everyone thought I had gotten married while on furlough because when I got my blouse ready to go to the cleaner's rice dumped out of the pocket!

Interestingly, I notice that whenever I come out of a building into bright sunlight I sneeze.

Thurs., 4.5.1945, Camp Bowie, Brownwood, Tex.
I know we're both happy about "us" but you seem to feel I'll stop loving you. Do you expect me to prove to be a first-class heel in the long run? I expect to spend the rest of my life with you.

My hands had been soft after a few weeks of clearing jams on the machine-gun ranges. Now they're full of burns, cuts and blisters.

Would you please send some airmail stamps?

We doubt that we'll be at Bowie for more than another month.

I don't think it would be hard to talk me into getting married the next time I'm home but even then, I'd expect you to stay in Baltimore. I feel strongly about wives following their husbands around to any camps.

Sun., 4.8.1945, Camp Bowie, Brownwood, Tex.
We drove 130 miles to Ft .Worth to have my photograph taken for you. Our unit is not "hot" but we've received a "warning" to have our equipment checked for combat serviceability. There is no place in "B-wood" to do it. Would have liked to have heard the Houston Symphony Orchestra with Oscar Lamont there but it was sold out. Will send the proofs to you to decide which you like best. I only

wanted one picture but the minimum order was of four. You started this so now it's your problem.

I'd like you to send a one-pound glass jar of "The Walnut" tobacco. My family sent one before when I was in Lake Charles.

Have you thrown away the envelopes from my letters yet? Don't you throw away anything?

Mon., 4.9.1945, U.S. Army Base Camp Bowie, Brownwood, Tex.
I must love you, I never seem to dream of anything anymore except you and those dreams cover everything from a wedding to washing dishes!

Wed., 4.11.1945, U.S. Army Base Camp Bowie, Brownwood, Tex.
Four of us are going to go to a school about war gas. The school starts on April 21st for a month near Denver. ___ says he's always liked Denver and the places around it. I will want you to send my camera to me once he finds out what my address will be there. Please send the camera, case, your case, sunshade and filter, color and black and white film, and the exposure meter.

I'm sending you some of the examples of wildflowers from the field near here.

We chased some armadillos today!

Sun., 4.15.1945, Camp Bowie, Brownwood, Tex.
What can I say? When you've just read two letters that tell you the girl you love so very dearly has missed you already, cried when you left, wishes we had married, and prays for your return. In the face of all that and feeling the same as you, it would seem foolish to write "It rained all yesterday and is still raining today" or "Got to camp 7:00 A.M. Sat. but they had my wire and everything was O.K."

Darling, the letter you had waiting for me when I got here is a masterpiece! If ever any woman has clearly expressed her love in a letter that was it! I was expecting a letter to be there when I arrived, but not such an honest, clear, heartwarming letter as it is. And then, a second letter and Easter card today.

Mer, I've seen people in love and I knew that love could be fine, but I never dreamed it could mean as much to me as it already does. You mean more to me than I could ever in any measure begin to tell you.

People keep asking, "Well, how was furlough?" You know how wonderful it was and so do I; but nobody else could ever understand what those few days were to us.

That October I thought we were as much in love as it was possible for any two persons to be, but now I see how mistaken I was. I don't know what the tie between us is that is so great, and I don't care as long as we never are without it.

I find that you have become everything to me. Days, nights, people, things no longer mean anything by themselves, but only their relation to you means anything to me. I love you, Mercia.
[Page itemizing second batch of slides and his comments on each one, presumably taken while on furlough]

Notice how we usually get 19 on an 18-exposure film? All in all, they are not too bad and not too good.

If I have a chance to use the camera around Colorado I'll try to use the exposure meter and also keep a record of the exposure and setting for each film and see if we can correct some of our errors.

Don't expect too much from those "pin ups" we took; as you'll notice none of those where we used the portrait lens seems to be very good.

I wish there were some way I could kiss you or hold your hand as well as talk to you. I'm still thinking too much and writing too little.

Mon., 4.16.1945, in the field, on letterhead reading Army Air Base, Lake Charles, LA (Crossed out)
Hope you don't mind too much about the stationary and lack of ink. This is all I had time to grab this AM when our whole outfit moved out in the field. We'll be out here roaming around in the trucks and trailers all week. At least the outfit will, but the four of us will have to go back into camp about the 18th to pack and leave for Denver.

I've been assured that the following address is OK so you may as well send the camera when you are ready: PFC AHN, Western Chemical Warfare School, Rocky Mountain Arsenal, Denver, Colorado
Don't worry too much about the packing as it won't break easily but you better insure it.

It's been a fine day to be outdoors today and I hope it keeps up. Everyone says my nose is red as W.C. Fields' now. We are in our trailer and cutting a fruitcake one fellow brought. You should see all the different methods of solving the housing and sleeping problem. Some have pitched their pup tents; some are sleeping in the backs of their trucks, some in the trailers, etc. My driver and I (gunner) are living in our trailer. It is small and cramped but is 10 feet long, four feet wide, and four feet high with a canvas roof. It's a lot better than a tent and we've folded the large canvas truck cover and put it on the floor of the trailer as a pad. So now, I'm in bed writing on a copy of *Coronet* with a floodlight stuck in the roof for light and eating fruitcake. Not bad! Then too, we are off the ground, which is a good point since about four rattlesnakes have been seen today. I even have a photo of you propped up.

Wed. 4.18.1945, Camp Bowie, Brownwood, Tex.
[Missing pages] We had been hoping they would let us leave for Denver a few days early because the outfit is going into

the field the 16th. However, it looks like we'll leave the 18th or 19th and have to go out in the field for two or three days. We may as well be out for the whole week as the packing and unpacking of equipment is the worst part anyway.

The "Iron Rabbit" was turned in, as we were never auth. to have one anyway.

The "Henpecked Lt." was trapped to another Q.N. outfit that lives next door. His replacement just arrived today and so far seems to be a good Joe.

Haven't had any classes to teach, but were on machine-gun range for two days. Spending most of my time now ordering parts for the guns we burnt-out and wrecked and wore out on the range.

I didn't mention the receipt of your willow caterpillar because I didn't receive it- 'til the day after I mentioned the subject. See-we do think of the same things don't we?

Glad to hear that you liked "The Robe" and I thought you would. But I don't see how on earth you finished it in two days. I know you read very rapidly, but after all! I don't see where you get time to read at all with all the work you do, letters you write, etc.

I don't read slowly by any means but I got a book a week ago and so far I've only had time to read 150 pages. It's "By Valor & Arms" about Civil War and not too good.

It's hot as hades here today and I don't think we'll go into suntans 'til the 23rd. I hope they'll let us leave here for Denver in suntans so we won't have to lug the wools around.

Thanks a millions for the stamps. You really are a dear. I love you quite a bit already and I'm doing better every day.

Thurs., 4.19.1945, Camp Bowie, Brownwood, Tex. George writes that he expects to be stateside in about another month.

The plan is to go from Camp Bowie to Santa Fe, change trains at Fort Worth and then onto Denver. We have reservations for Pullmans so the trip should be fairly comfortable.

My parents wrote that they are expecting George Jr. home for a few days before he leaves the States. His unit expects to be here until mid-August.

At the arsenal, we will be working with gas. Gas isn't as deadly as all the firearms I've played with. This is going to be more or less of a refresher course.

I've decided to go easy on the furloughs if I'm going to put aside money to get married. I didn't even get to church for Easter.

CHAPTER 3
Rocky Mountain Arsenal, Denver, Colorado

Sun. 4.22.1945, Rocky Mountain Arsenal, Denver, Col.
We spent three nights on a train and then when we got here we slept 'til noon.
On my way to the movies, I stopped in two PX's and no Camels. After the show, we stopped in the service club for a bite to eat and I found where they had the Camels so I got half a carton as per request, smoked my last pipeful of tobacco and went back to the barrack. There on my bed was a letter from you and something that looked like a time bomb. Your timing with that tobacco couldn't have been a bit better. I unwrapped it, filled my pipe and pouch and packed the jar in with my things for Denver. Then I used the cardboard and rubber bands you had used on the tobacco to wrap your Camels. That reminded me of when neighbors took cakes, etc. to someone their dish is usually returned filled instead of empty. It's a queer sort of war when you send me one kind of tobacco and I send you another. Maybe I should smoke more cigarettes and you should smoke a pipe.

The next AM half an hour before train time the orders were changed and one fellow was taken off the shipment. So at least the three of us got on the train and on our way. We had half hour at Fort Worth to change trains and to change stations. So, I grabbed a cab, dashed uptown to the studio, and had the cab wait for me and then take me over to the other railroad station. They retouched the photo to fix the back of the blouse and will print one 8 ½ in. x 10 in. and three 5 in. x 7 in. pictures. I didn't have too much time so I gave them your address and asked them to send all four to you. Two are going to my mother so could you see that she gets two of the smaller ones for Mother's Day for May 13th?

We were to have Pullmans, but the Army screwed up the reservations as usual and we didn't get them. However, it wasn't a bad trip and we had plenty of seats. At a town in Texas, a girl at a U.S.O. desk in the station said she'd mail the package for me. The trip was uneventful except that we got stalled for 2 ½ hrs. behind a broken-down freight out in the wilds of Texas. By the way, we're on Mountain Time now so there's two hours difference between us.

We went out to Walt O'Connell's house He's one of the three of us who came here and Denver is his home- how's that for a break? We think he'll be able to live at home and go to school here at the Arsenal. He may also get married while we're here. We met his mother where she works. (His father is dead.) She quit work early, went to the house with us, and fixed us a huge lunch while we shaved and cleaned up. Then the three of us went back to the station to wait for the Arsenal bus. Walt's girl was off work by then and she met us at the station and talked to us 'til we left. The arsenal is about 10 miles NE of Denver proper and is about a 34-minute bus ride. We live in a 2-story building with two men per room. I'm with Clyde Kelzer [Helzer], a Nebraska boy who was the other of the three. The rooms are nice: about 12 feet by 12 feet, 10 feet high, two beds, one window, one table, one lecture-arm chair, one closet. We were told that none of the rooms upstairs was filled and we'll probably have to fill them up and live one per room instead of two. That'll be nice in a way, but a sudden change when you are used to a barrack full of company. The schoolrooms, P.X., mess hall, quarters, etc. are all in a group so we don't have far to travel. We were told we can go to town every weeknight and are free weekends from 5 PM Sat. 'til 8 AM Mon. They gave us gate passes and told us we were free 'til Mon. AM. It seems that German PW's [Prisoners of War] pull all the K.P. and other details. Ain't it a hard life? Walt didn't wait to eat or fix his bed but took right off for home again. Can't blame him a bit. Clyde and I cleaned up and then went into town, wandered around a bit, then drank beer 'til we were about two sheets to the wind then came back here. It's nice to be able to go to a bar again and drink beer, or rye, etc. I guess they expect us to do some work here as when they gave us the blankets they also issued us each three different types of gas masks, but I think I'll have to take a lot of gas to make me dislike this setup.

Your photo was one of the first things I unpacked and it'll stay on the table beside my bed.

This will make my third spring this year. I saw spring come to Texas, then I moved north to see you and spring in Maryland, and now it's just starting here.

I wondered if there might be a ban on cameras here at the arsenal and I might have to leave it in town someplace; however, there is a notice that we many keep cameras if we register them with the school.

As for the armadillo, I heard that they roll up into a ball when caught; however, they don't seem to, nor do they fight. They simply start to dig and go underground. The boys carried one around and all it did was try to run at every chance.

On the truck-driving question, the latest joke is that one of our boys backed his truck into the side of Batt. Headquarters building and then tore half the boards off the place when he pulled away. The Colonel almost blew his stack!

It's too bad Walt's house isn't big enough that we could stay there on weekends, but, after all I guess we can't expect egg in our beer too! I even hoped we'd have a QX [Theta Chi fraternity] house in Denver, but no luck.

Mon., 4.23.1945 Rocky Mountain Arsenal, Denver, Col. Well, our first school day is over and not so bad. One thing- if I keep going to school while I'm in the Army it won't be so hard to go back to Law School. It looks like we'll have plenty to keep us busy as they gave us 19 (count 'em) books today! Chemistry, Weather, Flamethrowers, etc.

My record of my first winter without seeing snowfall was broken today. It snowed about two inches; however, it melted this noon and now there isn't a trace of it.

Walt completed arrangements today to live in town and is a glad guy. He also told us today to keep this Sun. open as he's going to get married then.

We start the day by getting up at 5:30 AM, breakfast at 7:00, and first class at 8:00 AM. Classes are 50 min. with a 10 min. break at the end of each. One hour for lunch and classes 'til 4:50 PM six days per week.

Clyde has already started to hit the books for tomorrow and says it's rough. They are really giving it to us thick and fast but then they say the first week is the worst.

Darling, you're not on a pink cloud…take it from your educated (?) fiancé that you are one bit of cumulus and possibly some cumulonimbus.

Armourer, gunner, gun instructor, assistant truck driver, chemical warfare instructor and metrologist. What the hell does Uncle Sam expect for only $54.00 a month?

Thurs., 4.26.1945, Rocky Mountain Arsenal, Denver, Col.

Still no sun today. We're beginning to wonder about this "*Springtime in the Rockies*" and *"Cool, comfortable, colorful Colorado*" action. We've been here five days now: had sun for one, clouds for one, rain for one and snow for two.

The Chemical Warfare (or Comical Warfare) School is where you have 19 beds, four gas masks and no free time. So far, we haven't tried to eat or shave with a gas mask on, but that's about all. Maybe the air is clear out here, but they clutter it up with all sorts of stuff.
Speaking of clear air, we sure noticed the change of altitude after Texas. Here we're just a mile above sea level and we're short-winded, pens leak easily, ears plug up, and a shaving

cut bleeds like a stuck pig. Once in a while, we think of you lovely mortals a mile below us.

By the way, I'll send more Camels to you in a few days. They are easy to get here and besides that they're only 10 cents per pack.

Had a letter from home today and George Jr. has gotten home. On the way, he drove his car all over trying to get a good price for it and finally sold it in New Orleans. He did OK 'tho as he paid $50.00 for it three years ago and sold it for $1,100!

I got my first burn and blister from the mustard gas. Don't get excited, it's only about the size of a dime and we all put some on each arm and then put the first aid ointment on one spot to be sure we react to mustard and the ointment-works OK.

Had a letter from Bud yesterday and also your letter with the note from Jane. Do you think the honeymoon is over now that they can both write? Bud says he'll send me an account of the honeymoon "with the natural exception of the more intimate details". I should think that would be mostly blank paper. But then-maybe I'm wrong.

Hear Lou Hatter has been moved to Fort Eustis, Va.

The family seems to think I'll be changing hat braid to chemical warfare now. I told them I was only a detached service. Come to think of it, I'm doing a good job of covering all the branches of the military.

I have to prepare a lecture-yes, still that. Among all the other stuff we also study "teaching methods", etc. and have to lecture once and awhile so we'll be able to teach this stuff when we get back (if we ever learn it ourselves) However only the basic things like mask drill, gas identification, and first aid will be taught and not all this weather, etc.

I tried to see if there was any sort of extension course I could take at Edgewood Arsenal [in MD], but no luck.

I seem to be smoking my pipe more lately with all my studies and it's good to have plenty of the "brand". It's holding out well 'tho as it should since it is a lot of tobacco and should last at least a half-year or 1/3 at my rate.

Sun., 4.29.1945, Rocky Mountain Arsenal, Denver, Col.
In the noon mail yesterday (Sat.) I got one package. When I saw it in the mailroom, I wasn't sure if it was the camera or film case. But I also realized one without the other wouldn't be any good, as even if I got the loaded camera I'd still need the orange filter. It turned out to be the film case. Usually the 5 PM mail is very light and we don't go over to check. But yesterday after I got the film I decided to check the evening mail. There was the camera. So, I unpacked it, read your notes, examined it and everything is fine. Then I registered it with the arsenal so now I'm all set to take it into town this afternoon.

In general, U.S. weather moves east and should reach Baltimore about two days after we have it here in Denver. 'Tho you'll get a little more rain, humidity, etc. you might sort of see if the weather you are having when you get my letters is about the same as it seems here when I wrote.

We went into town again last night and sopped up the beer. Just as we were waiting for the bus to go to town the news came thru that a V-E [Victory in Europe] flash had come thru and all it needed was to be declared official. Now the radio this AM says Truman has denied it. We got pretty well blotto last night and I have that dark brown taste, but I guess I'll live.

I wondered about your wedding dress last week when Walt's girl was talking about the one she bought. I know you'll look lovely and I hope and pray it won't be very long before I see you wearing it.

We've had two exams in the past week and yesterday those who flunked either or both were called to the Colonel's office. They just got "chewed" and those who flunked both (two men) were restricted from going to town for a week. None of our gang-Clyde, Walt or I made the Colonel's team so we're doing OK.

Your letters are so like you that they bring you very close to me.

Mon., 4.30.1945, Rocky Mountain Arsenal, Denver, Col. The weather again today was tops. This is the way we expected –"Cool, comfortable, colorful Colorado" to be. I guess you'd like to hear about the wedding wouldn't you? The plans were just started last week. The bride's (Doris Heck's [Hicks] mother is a WAC (and a very young looking one). (Between you and me, I'd rather go for her mother.) Her father is in the Navy so she was living with an aunt. Her mother got an emergency furlough and came home from Montana for the wedding. Walt O'Connell has a mother and 18 yr. old brother (father is dead). Walt's brother was best man and there were two ushers. Bride had two bride's maids and maid of honor. The girls wore different pastel dresses and carried sweetpeas. Men, except the groom, wore business suits. Let me prepare you by saying it was the longest wedding I've ever seen. (Baptist) From the time they went up to the aisle 'til they came back took exactly 25 minutes! First there was a solo. Then came the wedding march. Then, sort of tottering old minister who tried to preach a sermon at every chance. Several times, it seemed he was trying to talk them out of it, but it was a bit late for that. They went through several things at the altar and then just before the vows there was another solo while they just stood there. Her uncle gave her away. Everyone was almost asleep by the time they exchanged rings (double ring business that I'm not too devoted to). Then the groom kissed the bride (You know how I feel about that.) ...Everyone went to the groom's house for a dry reception. However, Clyde and I rode over with the drinking side of the family and we stopped for a snort on the way over. After the reception, they drove to a downtown hotel and stayed there. That was only last night and Walt had to get up at 6:00 AM to come to school- I told Clyde that I'd have at least got married Sat. night so I wouldn't have to get up at 6:00 the next morning!

Clyde just looked out the window and said the Kraut PW's are still working. There was a rumor that they were to start working on a 12-hour day. They're planting trees and making a lawn in the quadrangle.

Doubt I'll go to Colorado Springs alone and also not much to see as tourist season won't start 'til June as there's still too much snow on the mountain trails.

Tues., 5.1.1945, Rocky Mountain Arsenal, Denver, Col.
We don't have much on for tomorrow and we studied so much for the exam today that we deserve a rest. Besides we checked over the exam and I find I'll settle for a 90%, so one night off won't hurt.

Clyde and I are a bit worried about Walt 'tho. He's afraid he flunked and we're worried that they may make him live here instead of at the arsenal. We tried to cram him at noon today, but I don't know how well it worked. Also, on that score he told us that they got up at 5:00 AM today and moved from the hotel to an apt. they rented. The first AM of their married life they got up at 6:00 and the second AM at 5:00 AM! Isn't that a hell of a note?

Here's one that came up in class. Clothing to be worn around gas areas in chemically treated areas is impregnated so the chemical warfare outfits that do work are called "Impregnation Companies". Not long ago several WACs were assigned to those outfits and Col. Hobby raised such a fuss about her WACS being in "Impregnation Companies" that all had to be renamed "Processing Companies".

I never get tired of looking at these snow-capped mountains and I was thinking today that it seemed like a crime to have such scenery and weather when you aren't here with me. Towards the east, everything is flat and to the west are big snowy mountains. It seems there is always a bit of haze around the peaks, but you realize how clear the air is when you realize that the mountains seem about eight miles away and are really about forty!

I believe if I had known that the 470th would be here 'til August I would have wanted to get married on my last furlough. I didn't tell you did I that the morning we left Bowie one of our boys was killed when his jeep went off the road. He had only been married about three months and the fellows say that his wife (a WAC) is expecting!

Wed., 5.2.1945, Rocky Mountain Arsenal, Denver, Col.
Was thinking of Lake Charles when I first got the idea that I should ask you to marry me. Then the debates I had with myself as to if I was just lonely or not. And the decision to see how I felt after I had been home a few days. Then that Friday night in front of the Valley that I knew we were right. That busy Saturday AM with a ring to buy (it was picked out 'tho) and lots of things to do and meet you at noon at the "B'dere". I was a little late and hoped you wouldn't run into me in the hotel lobby. Gee, that box in my pocket seemed big! The football game…switching the box from one pocket to the other. Beating the crowd to the B'dere-all the time wondering when, where? Dinner at Marty's and the decision to stop at your office. Then in your office while I was searching for Bill's number I thought: here, now. "Sit down, I want to talk to you" –and it was as easy as that!

We just got back from a one-hour night display of wind. This new jeep bomb of jellied gasoline [napalm?] and __ and __ is quite the thing. We've seen it before, but the new class that came in last week was astounded. The new class is all naval officers. So now in the entire school we have about 41 G.I.'s (us; 45 Naval officers, and 20 Army Officers; Instructors). The Navy is paying more attention to chemical warfare since they had a bit of trouble in the C.B.I. [Believed to be China, Burma, and India]

Yes, we're wearing O.D.'s. They're warm some days, but feel good at night. Tonight for class half or so wore overcoats. We'll probably go into suntans May 15th and we go back to Texas on the 20th.

Don't worry about the gas masks. They all fit. They all protect against the same thing and are just different models in use now. One is the newest type and doesn't have any long snout-like hose. It just has the face piece with the can-like air filter on the left cheek. When we work in blister-gas areas, we're outfitted with all chemically treated clothes. Shoes, pants, shirts and even underwear and socks. Cotton gloves (treated) with rubber gloves over them. Masks, hoods, etc. Some of the outfits cover the body so much they can only be worn for an hour at a time.

Fri., 5.4.1945, Rocky Mountain Arsenal, Denver, Col.
There was a large-scale demonstration of bombing, rockets, smoke, etc. and they let us military come to see the show. Clyde has wanted to get into town while the stores were open to get his watch repaired so we made a quick change and hopped into town. Once you get there, the only buses that go to the arsenal in the evening are at 11:00 PM and 12:00 midnight. So, we got his watch fixed, drank some beer, had dinner, went to a movie, ate again, and then came back.

Now the rumor is making the rounds that when VE Day does arrive, that all soldiers will be restricted to their posts for three days. That's in order to try to keep them somewhat sober, from going AWOL, etc. If there's anything to it, maybe we should have got a quart or two to lay in the barracks just in case. It's a strange change from Texas to see signs in liquor stores here saying, "Buy by the case and save".

All three of us got thru the big exam we had last week. Clyde and I pulled down Ex (Excellent) and Walt got through with Very Satisfactory.

Yesterday they tried to make master plumbers out of us; learning to operate a smoke generator that vaporizes water and oil to make a fog. It's a plumber's delight. Then too, we had to make pipe connections to drain liquid agents from special containers. Today they tried to make demolition experts of us and we blew up bridges, mine fields, etc. and played around with blasting caps. Now they tell us we have to delve into the Interstate Commerce Reg. on railroad shipments of explosives and poison gas.

Sun., 5.6.1945, Rocky Mountain Arsenal, Denver, Col.
Last night Clyde and I went into town and had our normal binge. There was nothing unusual about it, just healthful relaxation. We also decided to stay in town for a change instead of dashing around to catch that last bus at 12:00. So we spent the night at the U.S.O. dorm, got up and had breakfast downtown, and then hitchhiked out to the arsenal in time for dinner. We're just starting to learn some of the nice bars, which way the streets run, what buses to take, etc. Just about the time we start to know our way around we'll have to leave. I guess next weekend will be our last in town as the return orders are usually for the Saturday that we finish school.

The business of when VE Day will be sure drags out. That would at least make it seem like we're getting somewhere with this war.

Tues., 5.8.1945, Rocky Mountain Arsenal, Denver, Col.
VE Day! I guess Baltimore was the same as Denver with fake VE Day rumors yesterday. In fact, about all the stores, etc. were closed in Denver yesterday. Then last night the radio said President Truman would make an address form Washington at 9:00 AM Eastern time this morning. So it came thru at 7:00 AM for us and we heard the good news just before breakfast. However, we had a rather normal day

with classes, exams, demonstrations, etc. Then at 3:00 PM, we all had to go up on the hill in front of the main arsenal building to hear speeches, etc. for an hour. Now all officers and men must stay here all night and can't get to town. I guess there'll be enough hell-raising without all the G.I.'s! But the day we want to see is the day when it will all be over. Walt is a little bit put out about not being able to go home to his wife of one week, but it won't kill him.

Clyde is sitting here polishing his buttons for the first time in his four years. Aren't I an influence on my friends?

We all seem to be passing our exams now. Walt flunked a quiz the other day but it wasn't a very important one. Two fellows flunked out and shipped back to their outfits yesterday so now we are 39 instead of 41. The class of naval officers left Saturday. (The Rocky Mountain Navy!) They only spent a week here and do not go into nearly the detail we do. Are spending a lot of time on flamethrowers this week and that's strictly roger with me!

Walt's wife went back to work after three days honeymoon. No, she'll stay here and Walt will go to Bowie without her and with us. The way things were set when we left Bowie the outfit will be out in the field almost all the time between our return and when the outfit takes off for lands unknown. And this VE business may mean that we'll leave sooner than we figured on at the last writing.

I guess by now you know what the Army at Occupied Germany will be. Or, in case you missed that bit of news, the 15th Army will occupy that part of Krautland that the U.S. will police. The 15th hasn't done any fighting, so I guess it is fairly fair. So I guess I won't get to Germany and that doesn't make me mad. Then too, Burma seems to be cleared of the little yellow ba---rds so I guess I won't get to go there either. That still doesn't make me mad. It seems my best bet is China, isn't it?

No, I didn't know that the film prepared for tropic shipment was black and white, but if it is it is. I won't worry about it just yet and I'll try to take a supply of color film with me. I have several rolls now and there seems to be plenty here in Denver.

Like a bolt out of the blue! "…twins or double bed?" she says sweetly! Well, it's this way, by the way, how come you didn't express your opinion on the subject instead of just asking? Here goes: As you know, I'm inclined to be considerate and 'tho I usually roll around, etc. I hate to when I sleep with someone for fear of disturbing that person (evaded that him or her, didn't I?) So, I always thought the twin beds would get my vote. BUT! - I could learn to like a double and since you know me, I will not need to go into reasons. So I vote for the double. But, I'm open to argument and I'd like to have your opinion on the matter. And, I mean, what was your opinion <u>before</u> I voted.

Walt just came back from the arsenal office. His aunt is telephone operator there and he went up to bat the ______. She reports Denver is quiet tonight and not any Army men except M.P.s in town. Even the general is still here at the arsenal instead of going home tonight.

What arrangement do I expect to make when it's over: This: 1) Return home and get a job, 2) marry you; 3) go to Univ. of Baltimore at night for one year and that'll finish the law. I couldn't finish sooner by going during the day because I'd have trouble changing my credits from Univ. of Baltimore to another school and Univ. of Baltimore doesn't have a day law school. If I work, we should be able to afford to be married since the G.I. Bill of Rights would pay for my school.

Wed. 5.9.1945, Rocky Mountain Arsenal, Denver, Col.
Had a letter from home today. Jr. got back to camp a day late, but with the usual "Naussberg" luck he got away with it. It seems their shipping orders have been delayed so they'll be around until at least the middle of May.

This noon they told us that the restriction was lifted and we could go to town this evening if we wish. Walt was happy and took off for home at 5:00 PM. I don't think we'll go to town 'til Sat. 'tho as we've quite a lot to study and an exam on Friday. Then too Clyde's blouse is in the cleaners and it's still too cool for suntans 'tho some do wear them.

Thurs., 5.10.1945, Rocky Mountain Arsenal, Denver, Col. It's a wonderful morning-not a cloud in the sky and just comfortably warm. Glad it's nice because we'll be outside almost all day today. 8:00-11:00 is outside firing the newest type of flamethrower. 11:000-12:00 is indoor class review for the big exam tomorrow. 1:00-5:00 will be outside work on decontaminating planes and tanks.

We just learned that the midnight curfew no longer applies and the brownout wasn't here to begin with. Better quit and locate the books to take to class. They just handed us seven more books! This makes a total of 20 books for a 30-day school!

Walt just got in from home and says to keep Sunday open as his mother wants us to come over for Sunday dinner. So Clyde and I just mulled it over and decided to try to get a hotel room and stay in town Saturday night instead of coming out Saturday night and going back in Sunday.

Had a lot of fun this morning firing the new flamethrower, mixing various fuels, etc. but this afternoon was rough. We were out decontaminating areas and equipment covered with mustard gas. The sun was bright and comfortably warm but the catch was that we had to spend three hours completely covered with masks and protective clothing. That meant wearing a full suit of <u>wool</u> <u>long-sleeved</u> underwear, chemically treated wool socks, leggings, coveralls, heavy cotton gloves, and also masks and large wool hoods. Then we had to work with all that on. It was brutal! Sweat would run down into your eyes and you couldn't do anything about it because of the mask. The removing all that clothing is an art in itself. We first remove masks and hand and rubber gloves and leave them outside the building. Then we enter and sit on long benches facing out and remove shoes and leggings-doing all this while keeping on the cotton gloves. Then shoes and leggings in a box, swing our legs over the bench, and put our feet down on the floor on the other side where shoes haven't touched. Next we undress completely still wearing gloves. The gloves are the last thing we remove before hitting the showers. Then a shower with strong G.I. soap to remove any trace of gas vapor and then into the next room and our own clothes.

Oh yes, points. All outfits have had a sealed copy to be shown on VE Day. However, there are so few military here that we didn't have a copy and got one from Lowery Field today. It explains who can expect to get out and how the point system will work for discharge. Just as we expected, most of us will be in this as long as Japan is. It's no use for me to try to explain it all…but all I have so far is about 30 points (one for each month service). The radio today said right now it takes at least 85 points and be unessential to get out. The 85 is hard enough but the unessential is the catch.

Here we are on that bed business again! I was glad to see that you "sort of ordered double" and since you couldn't have received my reply yet, we agree and your opinion wasn't influenced by my reply. Now our only trouble is how soon we'll get to use them!

Fri., 5.11.1945, Rocky Mountain Arsenal, Denver, Col.
We had our exam in the morning and there was nothing to it. When you come right down to it, there's nothing tough about the whole school if you study a little. But I guess that's only my point of view and most G.I.'s have been away from school longer than I and then too I've had a good bit more formal schooling than the average G.I. We lost another fellow yesterday but that only makes three out of 41 that started that have flunked out and shipped out.

Friday a week from today (May 18th) will be our last day at school. Then, if everything goes to plan, we'll leave here Saturday and get to Bowie Sunday night.

Speaking of Mother's Day-I wasn't speaking about it -but I was thinking about it. It seems in some way, or for some reason that you should be included. Does that sound foolish? I should have at least sent you a card inscribed "To the future mother of ~~my~~ our children". Maybe at this point I should stop and say I love you. I miss you day and night Mer, nearly every time I look at my watch I think of what time it is in Baltimore and what you must be doing.

It's late to get a reservation to stay in town tomorrow night; but last night we tried one hotel and they said call again tonight and tonight they said call at noon tomorrow, so we seem to be getting the runaround.

Tomorrow is a rough day. All classroom work and nothing outside. The worst of it is we have two out of eight hours with the poorest instructor in the school. He has days when we can hardly understand him. Can't understand why he's around when all the others are such good teachers.

Tues., 5.15.1945, Rocky Mountain Arsenal, Denver, Col. Clyde and I did our usual beer drinking Saturday night. This stag drinking isn't the best thing in the world, but it beats a blank and I can take it until I'm with you again. Then we spent the night at a hotel. Yes, we finally got a reservation. It was an old-fashioned place, but nice and clean. We slept 'til noon then had brunch, beat around downtown until about 2:00 PM and then went to Walt's mother's home. We had a fine dinner and spent the afternoon around the house with Mrs. O'Connell, Walt and Doris and Walt's 16 yr. old brother. Then in the evening, we all went to the movies. All the movies around here seem old. So as a result, Clyde and I didn't get to the arsenal 'til 1:00 AM Monday. We were in luck that we didn't have much in class today because neither of us cracked a book over the weekend.

I feel like a dog, not writing all day Saturday or Sunday, and getting such a nice letter from you today. And you were thoughtful enough to send more stamps too! I had just run out of them and hoped to be able to get some in town Saturday night but no luck.

A month ago we were talking to each other 'tho hundreds of miles apart. Two months before I was on a train speeding towards you. Seven months before I was putting a ring on your finger and kissing you.

I have tears in my eyes, but not over you. We spent the afternoon taking apart and repairing masks and then had to loaf around in the gas chamber to prove they still work. It doesn't bother you with the mask on, but the stuff hangs on our clothes and follows us around for an hour or two.

Well, four more days to go. We had our exam on "tactics" today and it was the roughest yet. There's an exam on "supply" tomorrow and then one on "gas protection" Friday. Saturday will be taken up with a tour thru the arsenal plant, graduation, and returning masks, etc. We've still not been able to get any advance dope on leaving, but it'll probably be Sat. or Sun.

Here's one for the records! Yours truly refused his pay! Today they made up a payroll for us and I wouldn't take mine! About three months ago, I made out a class E allotment (just an arrangement to send home $25.00 per month for deposit). Mother writes that she has received two checks of $50.00 and as yet they haven't deducted anything from my pay! Since I have enough to last about two months I decided not to take this pay and get it straightened out because now I'm $50.00 ahead of the government and I may as well clear it up now as let it ride and then not draw my pay for several months.

I'm glad you mentioned the fact that I may not pass the bar exam the first year, because that is <u>very</u> possible.

Wed., 5.16.1945, Rocky Mountain Arsenal, Denver, Col. ...Speaking of photos- I took the first five on the new roll of color film. I was working under a handicap but I still think they'll be good. About 15 of us were on an assault team to assault a pillbox of logs. As a result, I was firing a bazooka and taking photos of the flame-throwers in action. You can realize how busy I was when you realize that a flamethrower only operates for nine seconds before it runs out of fuel. Then too, I had to photograph 'thru spaces in a smoke screen! I think I got three good ones and I think I skipped one frame. Then for the fifth, I took one of Clyde in a new type combat mask.

All three of us passed our exams yesterday and today. This AM everyone was talking about the huge amount of noise some of the fellows made around 1:00 AM when they came in tanked. I seem to be the only one who slept thru it and didn't hear a sound. Clyde says they even pounded on our door.

Thurs. 5.17.1945, Rocky Mountain Arsenal, Denver, Col. "*Tis a privilege to live in Colorado!*" Dearest Vixen, today was another one of those days that made one realize why the above motto is seen everywhere! The snow on the mountains seemed close enough for about a 10 min. drive and it was just warm enough for comfort. The more we think about it the more we hate to go back to Bowie. But then, this isn't an old soldier's home and there's work to be done.

This noon we were out on a problem to decontaminate our way thru grass covered with mustard gas and it backfired. All went well for the first three methods we used. But, the fourth way was to burn a path clear with flamethrowers. Well, the wind changed at just the wrong time and started the darndest brush fire you want to see! We used 800 gal. of water from a pumping truck and I don't know how many hand grenades before we got it out. And the worst of it was that the gas-filled smoke was blowing back on us all the time. As soon as we got back, we all jammed into the showers and now we'll wait 5-10 hrs. to see if we develop any vapor burns. We're not worried 'tho as vapor burns are just like sunburn. Clyde and I have our clothes hanging out the window to air.

Here's the latest dope on our leaving, hot off the board: Graduation will be over at 4:00 PM Sat. and everyone will leave between then and Mon. noon depending on where he's going. Clyde, Walt, and I are to catch the 7:00 PM train Sat. That's getting us out quickly, isn't it? Maybe they don't love us as much as we thought they did.

We had our last and largest exam today, the one that can fail you on the course if you flunk that one alone. However, we understood we all passed except one man and he was called over to see Col. this evening. Tomorrow evening (Fri.), we're having a class party at a gin mill just outside the arsenal reservation- object- to get "stinkin' from drinkin'"! We will all probably be in rare shape for the tour of the arsenal plant and graduation Saturday.

The worst part of our leaving Sat. is that we think the 470th is to go out into the field for three weeks starting Mon. I'll bet we'll get in Sun. eve. And just have time to grab some stuff and go out with the boys. Oh well.

Have you had to pay postage on any of the shipments I've sent? We usually can't get to a post office so we'll just have to estimate the postage and drop the package into a mailbox.

You can do things to me with only a letter that I never thought you would be able to do.

Clyde just reported that a Sgt. down the hall has discovered a 6-inch square of "sunburn" on his back. I guess we'll all start hunting for patches now 'tho if we find any, the only thing to do is wait a few days 'til they go away. Doubt if any will get blisters 'tho.

One of these days you'll be quite an authority on pipe supplies won't you? Couldn't dream what was in that letter! I stuck it in my pocket and used it all afternoon. The tamper end works better than my pen and is better for the pen. I even found out that the needle thing serves well to put a clogged flamethrower back into operation.

Frank surely writes a good letter, doesn't he? It must be a rough go over there and I hope he makes the grade OK. I bet his letters sound just like he talks. Don't worry about his use of profanity- that's the Army and we all get that way from men living together too much. But I think we'll all recover when we're civilians again and around those we love.

Just checked me over and no burns (yet). I'll bet Walt has some as this stuff really bothers him.

CHAPTER 4
Back to Camp Bowie, Brownwood, Texas

Fri., 5.18.1945, Camp Bowie, Brownwood, Tex.
Well, as you can see we made it back again. And how we wish we could turn right around and go back to Colorado!

We had a class party at the "Curve Inn" Fri. night and a good time was had by all. We drank quite a few, but everyone held it very well. We were a lot of sad sacks Sat. 'tho and all looked like we should go to the blood bank and have our eyes drained! By luck we only had one lecture on Sat. because during that hour one fellow counted 19 out of 36 asleep at one time! We managed to drag ourselves thru the day and then had graduation at 3:30 PM. The Col. made it short and sweet ('til Allen was cited as being one of the top three) and by 4:30 PM we were down at the station. Our train was 7:00 PM so Walt took off for home and Clyde and I got dinner downtown. Our train was a slow milk run due here at 4:30 AM Mon. and we tried to change to the Zypher that would let us stay over Sat. night-leave 1:00 PM Sun. and still got here the same time. However, we weren't able to change because of the Pullman. The first night we had a troop sleeper (three high) that was only half-full and we were very comfortable, except for the fact that we began to feel the Texas heat and changed from O.D.'s to suntans en route. I had wrapped a package of cards for you before we left and when we got to the station I couldn't find it. When we changed uniforms, I found it on the bottom of my bag and mailed it in Fort Worth. We kept ourselves amused on the train with highballs (it's handy to like plain water) and a bit of beer in Fort Worth during our two hours between trains. We left Fort Worth at 11:25 PM and went right to bed. This time we had four uppers in an ordinary Pullman. There were four of us as one was sent from another company in our batt. Remember four of us were to go and they scratched one fellow at the last minute?

We had to get up at the weird hour of 4:15 AM to get off at B-wood and it was raining hard! We had breakfast and got to camp about 7:00 AM to find everyone out in the field. So we've spent until now cleaning up, unpacking and packing up our field equipment. They've been out there one week, which means we'll have two weeks in the field more.

We haven't been around long enough to get posted on the latest dope, but so far as we can gather the outfits still expect to pull out around the middle of Aug.-and there is almost no chance that I'll get home again before we leave.

Wed., 5.23.1945, Camp Bowie, Brownwood, Tex.
This is a sad-looking piece of paper to use for a letter, but we're in the field and I've been carrying it in my helmet for two days waiting for a chance to write.

I have a new job now- but it'll only last 24 hours and that's plenty. I'm now a switchboard operator! Yes, I know, Jack-Of-All-Trades and master of none. All four of our companies are out here in the field and Batt. H.Q. had to leave for a 24-hour problem and two of us had to take over and work the board. I've never worked one before, but they said it was easy to learn and you know me- the eager beaver stays ready to learn something new. This job isn't bad for 24 hours but would drive me bats for a longer period. The line from Bowie out here is on the fritz and Bowie can call us, but we can't call them. So meanwhile, we have Bowie call every 20 min. when we have an outgoing call. There's a lineman trying to fix it now. Then too, people keep calling Batt. HQ and I have to explain that they all pulled out on their problem and the switchboard and I are all that remain. They can have this job. It's bad enough to belong to one of those screwball outfits, but to try to keep them in touch with each other is too much.

This other fellow and I have to stay out here in the middle of nowhere 'til noon tomorrow to operate this board. It won't be so bad since we've located six potatoes to bake and three quarts of milk.

It seems one or two of your letters that arrived here lately were forwarded to Denver and will have to be forwarded back again.

Fri., 5.25.1945, Camp Bowie, Brownwood, Tex.
I've just finished breakfast and am sitting on a rack (flat) and leaning against a tree. I'm using my gas mask (with camera inside) as a desk. It's non-reg. to carry extra stuff in a mask, but that's the only way to always have the camera with me and since I'm now the "gas expert" I can get away with it.

Had to relieve a guard this morning so he could eat, so I missed going out on a short hike with the boys, but they are coming back in now.

Too many ticks and chiggers and snakes around so I've been using my tent as a hammock.

Sun., 5.27.1945, Camp Bowie, Brownwood, Tex.
You can't sleep on your face in a hammock! (I look better that way) so I tried it last night and almost broke my back!

I see now the back of this mess kit makes a poor desk, but it'll have to do. This life in the field isn't too bad after you get used to it, but there are better ways to live.

My bank balance took quite a beating with furloughs, ring, etc. but I don't regret a bit of it I'm not putting any more into bonds now as we'll need the cash. That's the picture- just a pair of church mice aren't we?

In a letter from home I just learned Elliott Harwood hit the States in April. He's in Woodrow Wilson Hospital in Staunton, VA with wounds he picked up in the islands.
Here's where I brag a bit, but don't get your hopes up. As I told you I was in the top three at Denver. Well my rating on Chem. War. was "Superior" and my rating as an instructor was "Excellent". So now it seems that the school sent down a letter of commendation on me and our colonel saw it and told our Capt. "That man should be made a Cpl. as soon as you have an opening." The trouble with that as there has been all along, is

we, as almost all outfits in the States, are already over-rated and there is seldom an opening. That's known as "T.S.".

According to reports our outfit is getting better and better every day. It seems now we have top prior rating to order any type of equipment we need.

I know just what you mean when you say you have trouble getting in touch with my mother. She does get around a bit doesn't she? Now you see why my brother and I each carried a door key ever since we were tall enough to reach the doorknob!

Speaking of food the boys tell me that the first week here in the field a few of them caught an armadillo and cooked armadillo steaks just to see how it was. They said it was really good, but somehow the idea doesn't appeal to me. But then some of this gang will eat anything that doesn't bite them first. If I had had just one cartridge for my carbine handy when I got out of bed this AM we could have had roast pheasant today.

I could wire a light from the truck battery over my hammock (all the comforts of home) but the mosquitoes like the idea so much that I refuse to do it.
Goodnight darling. Again tonight I'll lay here and look at the full moon and think of: Mercia, Mer, Vixen, my best girl, my fiancée, my future wife.

Mon., 5.28.1945, Camp Bowie, Brownwood, Tex.
In the field it seems you spend more time getting to do things than doing them. I just finished shaving and 'tho your washstand is wherever you put your helmet, you still have to unpack razor, soap, etc. and get water. At least we have some comforts that foot troops don't here. A G.I. truck fender is the right height for a washstand and the side mirror makes a good shaving mirror.

We got hold of a gasoline powered generator so we'll have a movie tonight as soon as it gets dark.

I wish Yardley [*Baltimore Sun* cartoonist] wouldn't draw cartoons about Ocean City [MD]-it almost breaks my heart. I had sort of hoped against hope that I'd be able to get a furlough when you had your vacation and we'd be able to spend a week at Ocean City together. But, pipe dreams!

My hammock arrangement works wonderfully well. It's really a truck tarp- the large canvas cover and folded 'til it's about four feet wide. So it really doesn't swing and it's only claim to being a hammock is the middle sag. I even have a canvas roof to roll out now in case of rain. Then too this whole truck that I'm using as my quarters is under a huge camouflage net that is the size of a small circus tent. The mesh is about ½ in. x ¼ in. so it at least keeps out the tri-motor mosquitoes.

Today we got in some new type anti-air machine gun mounts and were setting them up and lo and behold they were made in Philadelphia and stamped over with "Phila. Ordnance Dist.,"-my old home office-all it lacked was "Balto. Sub. Off."
Glad to hear that you got the shipment of weeds [cigarettes]. They'll be a little harder to get around here.

Thurs., 5.31.1945, Camp Bowie, Brownwood, Tex., in the field
I'm so dirty right now that I feel hardly fit to write to you. Everything around here is just dust, dust, dust. We left yesterday noon on a training test problem and got back at noon today; tired and plenty dirty and no chance to get my sleep all night. We did pretty well 'tho, covered over 150 miles of complete blackout _____ with 35 trucks and didn't have a single accident. The dust caked on our faces around our goggles and dust respirators so much that most of us changed and wore gas masks instead.

As far as we know we'll go back to camp this Sat. night or Sun. and after that your mail will be a little more regular, I hope.

Do you know yet when you'll take your vacation and do you have any plans or hopes as to what you'll do? Thanks a million for the room-plan. Now I can dream of you just a little more clearly- every little bit helps.

No dear, I don't need tobacco yet! In fact I'm not half finished the jar you sent.

Don't worry about the bridge! In the past two years I've only played once, so you'll probably have to teach me or we'll learn together.

Just felt a few drops of rain and must rig a tent canopy over my bunk or my hammock will bill up like a bathtub- on second thought that's an idea since I need a bath anyway.

Fri., 6.1.1945, Camp Bowie, Brownwood, Tex.
My father was elected chairman of the Baltimore Chapter of the American Society of Metals. He was also chairman of the Washington Chapter before there was one in Baltimore.

I've shaved off the hair adornment to my upper lip.

Our alert day has been moved to June 29th from July 10th.

Sat., 6.2.1945, Fort Worth, Tex.
Most of our times together seem to have been in the spring or fall, don't they? But I still think of three of our hot weather dates. "The Anchorage" where the first night I met you and played wolf and made a date (also the man tried to throw his wife over the rail into the water); then just riding at night in the country; then I always recall with a sheepish grin the time I took you and Sis [Eleanor Stratton] swimming. Sometime I'll have to take you out there <u>alone</u> just to make up for that.

Our alert date has been set for July 10th but our P.O.E. date still will be around the middle to August, probably to California.
[Cartoon of groom proposing to his bride enclosed]

Tues., 6.5.1945, Camp Bowie, Brownwood, Tex.
My mother was surprised that I bought your ring before I asked you to marry me.
I've decided to grow a moustache-it's red…

Thurs., 6.7.1945, Camp Bowie, Brownwood, Tex.
Please assure your boss that I don't think I'll be able to get home until the war is over.

Sun., 6.10.1945, Camp Bowie, Brownwood, Tex. letterhead
Last night around midnight it started to rain and we thought the wind would blow the roof off. It was just about like the winds at Camp Houge. We had to close all the windows and that brought up a problem. A bird built a nest on the sill of one window at the end of the barrack that props open and in the nest for the past three days there has been a tiny white egg. Needless to say, we've all been watching the progress of the nest, bird, and egg just outside our screen. So, when the wind started to blow we knew that unless we closed the window the nest and egg would blow off the sill-but the mother bird wasn't around and if we closed the window she couldn't get to the nest until the window was opened again. Can't you just see eight supposed hard-bitten G.I.s sitting on the end of their bunks at midnight debating what to do. We finally decided to close it and this AM when we opened it the mother bird was excitedly back. I tried to get a photo of the nest today. I've taken very few. It seems there's nothing worth taking around here. I would like to use up the camera film before leaving the States. I won't take the filters, sunshade, or meter, just the camera and film.

Finally got my payroll straightened out and in doing so drew a $5.00 bill of the invasion money with "Hawaii" written across the back. Otherwise, it's just the same as any other five. I hear there's a lot of it floating around the West Coast.

I've beat you on the swimming, in fact I've been in four times this past week. (Army life is rough isn't it?) But then it's even less trouble to walk to the pool in the evening than to the movie and it doesn't cost anything. I'm a regular Scotsman-I've had those trunks for 4-5 years and the seams keep coming apart. I'd gladly throw them away if I could buy a pair as good-but I can't. I've already replaced over half of the seams and it looks like what's known as "saddle stitching" but it does the job.

It seems that the troops that go near the end of the war will probably end up as occupation troops so we're hoping to go sooner rather than later.

I wouldn't want you to come to Texas. I know just how it would be. I'd get a few days off; we'd decide to get married, and then have to leave each other after only a few days. Then we'd kid ourselves that we had done the right thing. We'll wait and do it right. You just stay there sweetheart and write and one of these days I'll come home to you to stay and we'll be married and live happily ever after.

Wed., 6.13.1945, U.S. Army Camp Bowie, Brownwood, Tex. Forty-eight hours without having my clothes off is pretty busy for camp life. Early Tuesday morning we had another problem- this time without trucks. We had to hole out about 10 miles, set up a bivouac, fool around and spend the night there. What a night that was! We had to use these blasted pup tents and as luck would have it we had a Texas flash flood. It rained hard, the wind blew, and then we had a hailstorm! Some of the hail even went right thru the tents, etc. Then on top of our troubles, the 4th Army pulled a surprise inspection on our trucks and gigged everything in sight- so we all had to work 'til 10 PM last night on them. So that, along with almost no sleep the night before made me so tired that we all just lay down and went to sleep without even taking our clothes off. Then too we have a raft of packing cases all ready to start packing our equipment to take on the boat.

I only wish I could do nearly a well writing to you as you do to me. When I have spare time I even stamp and address several envelopes in advance, but I still get behind quite often. We don't even seem to have a lunch hour anymore. We just had to go over to the medics for more "shots" I protested and when they checked my records they found I was up to date. The rest are still over there getting one, two, or three.

Our bird's nest on the window sill has two eggs now. I think it was only one when I wrote last.

Remember how I disliked the photo you sent me at Yale? That's the one I keep on my shelf now and I realize the "feather cut" would be cooler in summer and perhaps easier to manage, but I do prefer the "page boy"

I know it's all very involved- do I go to school or field problems, etc. That's typical of this screwed up outfit. We have so many men in school, furloughs, etc. that when a field problem comes up they yank us out of school for the day in order to have more than a mere handful of men.

No, I'm not so set on meeting the Hendersons. In fact I'm more on the alert or grasping at the straw of an idea that by some strange chance I might get home before we leave. I even keep at least $50 in cash so I'll be sure to have fare on a moment's notice. Not much hope, but they can't shoot you for hoping.

I was thinking about the stock of film. I have two 18-exposure rolls of black and white and two of color. But one of the color rolls is for indoors and I don't expect to take the filters, etc. overseas, so I'd better use the indoor one before we hit ship. Black and white may be better because of having them developed to be censored, etc. and also for fellows who want prints. So I'd like you to try to send me two rolls of color (outdoor) and two rolls of black and white 36-exposure would be better as I'd have more film in the same amount of space. But- if you do arrange to send the films, I also want you to be sure to send me the bill.

The moustache is small and thin, but too much trouble shaving and think I'll quit. You wouldn't even be able to see it on a picture.

Sun., 6.17.1945, Camp Bowie, Brownwood, Tex.
Taking up sewing again- becoming quite the little future housewife aren't you? Glad to hear it, gal. I'm looking forward to the day when I'll have you to sew a button on my shirt instead of doing it myself. A yellow bathing suit! Maybe we should cut the camera in half so each of us can have it. I think I'd like the

suit- I usually like your clothes, with the exception of the hat with wings! I'll never let you forget that.

The leather came yesterday and you sure did save every scrap didn't you? There is plenty of leather there and I should be able to get along and not even use the large piece. I always want something don't I? Now I need two snap fasteners. Could you be so kind-you are a dear you know. I'll need time, but I'll send you any leather that remains that is worth saving. I save some things, but not nearly as much as you.

It seems settled now that Seattle will be our P.O.E. If they keep moving our date up and George's date back I may have a chance to run into him yet.

What about that Father's Day card? My reaction could be "Why didn't you tell me- I didn't know!" But knowing you as I do I guess you sent it even 'tho it didn't quite apply. A thing like that could worry a single man you know.

Tues., 6.19.1945, Camp Bowie, Brownwood, Tex.
My letters have been pretty few and far between since I got back to Bowie. There are so many in school and on furlough that we have to work about every evening packing and marking cases of guns, clothes, etc.

The other night we had a radio going in the supply room while we were working, and we heard Walter Hamden playing "Cyrano". That play has always been one of my favorites I guess because it was about the first thing that I read in French and then I saw it on stage with Hampden soon after.

We go to school, pack stuff at night and then take time off from school to go into the field. We're going out in the field again tomorrow and will come back in about noon the next day. I hope we don't have any hailstorms this trip.

Have been chewing the fat with a few camera bugs in the outfit and we may try to take chemicals, etc. with us and develop and print our black and white films. India, China, Russia, the islands-where are we going? Don't we wonder and don't we wish we knew?

Wed., 6.20.1945, Camp Bowie, Brownwood, Tex.
We had a gas alarm. We are used to wearing our masks now. It's frustrating, the only times I've felt like I was doing something useful were with traffic control at the Pentagon building armoury and at Lake Charles and neither of those compared to when I was a civilian ordnance inspector.
Do either you or Jo know how to make mint juleps? I haven't indulged enough to develop an opinion on whether I prefer bruised or untouched mint.

So, you are having the ring engraved. That's like saying "it's going to be a long engagement". "V to V'en 10-14-44". I'm glad you have the QX [Theta Chi] pin as well. You ask what the middle initial in my father's G.M.N. is-the middle name of my father's mother's name- MURRY [sic Murray] a good old Irish name.

Sun., 6.24.1945, Fort Worth, Tex., Fort Worth Service Men's Centers stationary
Need I say I'm in Fort Worth? The stationary doesn't seem very modest about it, does it?

We've all been working like beavers lately and almost doing without sleep. However now we've turned in all the trucks and drawn a good bit of our overseas clothing and packed about half of the guns and stuff.

Yesterday morning we had an inspection by a group of Washington bigwigs. We must have impressed them because it was hardly over at noon Sat. when the 7th Headquarters of 4th Army called and said the men deserved a rest and 100% of the men could go on pass until Tues AM! It's unusual enough to get all day Monday off, but it's even more unusual to allow 100% of an outfit to leave all at one time. At any rate, four of us got an official OK to drive a jeep to Fort Worth and here we are. We had to park the jeep in front of M.P. Hq. and can't use it to tour around town, but it was a break to be able to us it for the trip.

I just dashed over to tell two fellows from 470th that we're off 'til Tues. We did not get the official work until about 4:00 PM and a lot of fellows had already left camp with the idea that they had to be back Monday.

Our bird's nest no longer has the two eggs- it has two small birds now.

We drank our troubles away last night and didn't catch up on any sleep-in fact we lost more. We've been in sort of a fog all day. We went to a movie this afternoon and I fell asleep twice. After the movie we had a large seafood (it's so novel for soldiers) dinner with wine and all the trimmings. I could sleep for a week now.

Am beating around with Dave Bush. He's nice, from West Coast (L.A.) just returned from furlough and is in the same fix as I; he expects to wait until after the war to get married and wonders if he should have married the girl while he was home. So both feeling as we do, we can have a good time in town, without bothering about women-so cast your fears aside.

Tues., 6.26.1945, Camp Bowie, Brownwood, Tex.
We are alerted for leaving on the 29th and will leave five to ten days after the advance party leaves.

I haven't gotten to buy your cigarettes yet.

You talk about Cape May. I've always gone to Ocean City [MD] and never to Cape May [NJ].

Sun., 7.1.1945, Camp Bowie, Brownwood, Tex.
I sent you a birthday gift but I'm not sure you will know what it is so I will write to you to explain. I don't want you to open your birthday gift until your birthday. You are not to shake it or you might break them. You are the only one for me and will always be. I can do without other girls. Please don't write "If you love

me enough…" I don't want you to ever feel even the slightest "if" about my love for you.

Young love is really something! Walt O'Connell has only been back from furlough a little over a week and just got a wire that his wife Doris is on her way down here. She knows that we may move out any day now and that all the married men have just sent their wives home and yet now she quit her job and starts down! I think love is wonderful and all that, but I did give the girl credit for more sense than that and Walt says that he tried to talk her out of coming down.

The fellow I went swimming with today is here now rubbing boric acid ointment on his sunburn. I can't see any difference in my color, but he hasn't been out often and is red as a lobster.

One of the few remaining seams on my trunks that I hadn't repaired gave way today. I guess your bathing suit is finished now- but I'm still sewing on mine.

I didn't know until I was told that two divisions are due to arrive from E.T.O. [European Theater of Operations] to train for the Pacific.

Thurs., 7.5.1945, Camp Bowie, Brownwood, Tex.
Lent my pen to one of the boys yesterday and he forgot and took it into town with him for the weekend. I had an addressed envelope, so at least that much will be in ink.

I did some shopping in B'wood and finally selected your birthday gift. It's a little early, but with the possibility of shipping out, I didn't want to leave it until the last minute. The salesgirl said she wouldn't mail it until about the end of the week, so as to be nearer to the 25th. But it will still be somewhat ahead of time and I don't want you to open it until your birthday! What's more, don't keep shaking it or you might break it or rather them.

This morning we saw one of our small birds walking around on the windowsill outside of the nest. Then this noon the nest was empty and still is, so they must have taken right off. That makes just ten days since the eggs hatched.

I had a swim for about two hours this afternoon and now we're having a thunderstorm so I haven't minded the heat that much today.

The day was just like all the others and in the evening, Dave, Bud and I went in to Brownwood to a movie.

There is still no change in our status, so still we wait. Rumors are thick and fast 'tho.
The family doesn't seem to have gotten my letter explaining that we were alerted for the 29th and not to leave then. They seem to have me on the way to Seattle already with "Please Forward" on my mail and all that. I should be able to let you both know about a week to five days before we really leave.

A few of us have to put up some sort of chemical display in the morning and I'll have to find out what it's all about.

Tues., 7.3.1945, Camp Bowie, Brownwood, Tex.
Word is that maybe our priority has been dragged so low that we'll be here for three months or that our unit may be disbanded.

I was looking for a walnut pipe tobacco but maybe you could send me some. I can't believe you have never heard of cantaloupe and ice cream. You fill a half cantaloupe with the ice cream and eat it together. I've been quitting both smoking and drinking for a couple of weeks at a time off and on now just to make sure I still can quit.

Fri., 7.6.1945, Camp Bowie, Brownwood, Tex.
Love letters during duty hours- that shows how busy we are just now. They've run so low on things for us to do (and it's raining) that we were given this time to pack up stuff we want to send home. If we send it now it will go at gov't expense. However, about all I'll send home are my civilian shoes and my moccasins. And for those I'll wait and not send them until the advance party

leaves. Because who knows we may be here for a month or so yet.

They're starting to have refresher classes in map reading, etc. but can't do much except kill time because everything is packed up. We can't even go out in the rain without getting wet because all our raincoats have been turned in. Overseas we'll wear ponchos and they're all new and packed in our duffle bags.

No letter yesterday, but you sure caught up with the eight-page sugar report that came today.

Last night I got around to cutting out the first part of the watch strap. You'd think I was drunk the way it looks and I'll have to try again. Maybe if I keep doing that badly I will need all that leather that you sent after all.

I finally completed the film that I started just before we left Denver. I hope this will give better results than ones of Walt's wedding.

What a crew this is! Thirteen of us sleep here and right now six are sound asleep, two of us are writing and one is reading. I don't know where the others are, but it's an even bet they're asleep somewhere. This army life is tough! I wonder what the poor people are doing this afternoon. Hold it- another just came in and hit the sack-that makes seven asleep! Rough! And the radio just bleats its brains out without anyone paying attention, but everybody is too lazy to turn it off.

Yes, Clyde Helzer and Walt O'Connell are still here. Walt's wife just got here last weekend from Denver and he's living in B-wood now. Dave Bush had an impulse yesterday and shaved off his mustache. He's worn one ever since we've known him and he doesn't look like the same person without it. He's the youngest fellow in the outfit (21) and looks like it now. He wears glasses, always smokes a pipe and the thick, bushy mustache made him look like a professor of 30 before. I like him better with it and I'm trying to get him to let it grow again. He's been working for three days on A.P.O. notice cards to be sent out from Seattle.

No, no, the dog tags only have to be worn during duty hours and not to bed. They also are neither cold nor hot-now that I have rubber edges around them and that cuts down on the noise and cold metal feeling.

Dave Bush and I are thinking about running down to San Antonio if we get off at noon tomorrow.

Sun., 7.8.1945, [Two postcards from San Antonio, one of the Alamo and one of San Jose Mission, one card to Mercia at home and the other to her workplace.
Walked our legs off but seeing lots of sights. You'll see the pictures.

Mon., 7.9.1945, Camp Bowie, Brownwood, Tex.
Dave Bush and I spent the weekend in San Antonio and visited the Alamo. I was able to take some color photos that I will send. The base is about 180 miles from the city and we hitchhiked there and back. It's somewhere near Abilene Air Base.

I hide my face in shame that the "Naussberg" mariner has slipped as far that I had to be even gently reminded to write Aunt Kate.

Tues., 7.10.1945, Camp Bowie, Brownwood, Tex.

"*A Journey to San Antonio*"

The following is a true account of the daring trip by David Bush and Allen Nauss into the barbaric wilds of Texas.

At 6:00 AM Saturday, 7 July 1945 we were awakened by a terrific downpour that quickly took the form of a flash flood. All barracks were above the ground level and escaped damage, but ten inches of water covered the floor of the dayroom.

By 11:00 the rain had ceased and patches of blue sky showed the prospect of fair weather. At lunch Dave Bush came to me and said; "Do you think we should try to hitch-hike to San Antonio even 'tho we don't have raincoats?"

"Sure, I'm for it, even 'tho it is 188 miles."

By 1:00 PM we had showered, shaved, and were on our way. It wasn't necessary to go to Brownwood as we were heading south and the camp is south of town. We went out to highway #U.S. 283 and waited- and waited. We waited one full hour and were passed by quite a few cars before we were picked up by two ranchers in a small pick-up truck with three other G.I.'s riding in the back. This, our first ride was good for 47 miles-to the town of Brady, Texas; and uneventful with the exception of one blowout. The other three G.I.'s were staying in Brady and expressed the view that; "It takes nerve to go as far as San Antonio on a weekend pass."

At this point it might be well to clarify the name of our objective. People other than Texans refer to "San-Anne-tone-e-oh" cowboys and hillbillies sing of "Sanantone". It is well to note that a story by O'Henry carried the name of "Sanantone". The natives of the fair city call it "San Antono""-and they should know.

On the outskirts of Brady we again had a long wait while our faith in humanity sank lower and lower. It should be clear that those who have the least to offer are often most willing to share with others. An old farmer with a pick-up truck dragged to a stop and offered a ride to the town of Mason. There were two G.I.'s in the front seat and two evil looking goats in the back of the truck. Our morale <u>was</u> low, but nevertheless we declined to ride with the goats. A short time after the goats had passed a large Buick picked us up. The man was "going up the road a piece to deliver a tire."

We flew low at 70 M.P.H. for about 20 miles and reached a small oil truck on the side of the road. After the tire had been changed the Buick returned to Brady and the oil truck took us on beyond Mason. The oil truck ride ended at a small side road and left us on the highway with not a building in sight.

The next car to stop was a state police patrol car! The trooper inquired who we were, why we were there, and where we were going. "You'll pick up a ride soon."-and he was off-in our direction and with an empty car, but without us!

Then our truck appeared! A large truck with crude, long, flat, homemade trailer affair. The truck seat was occupied by two bearded men and a plain woman of about thirty with a small baby in her arms. Back on the trailer a youth of seventeen was riding on a pile of quilts.

"Where you'all goin'?" "San Antonio" "Climb aboard, so are we!"

The oceans are rough; war is rough; but so was that trailer. There were many stops to change the baby, get the baby's bottle and check the tires. At each stop Dave and I also looked at the wheels to assure ourselves that the wheels weren't square after all. Our hosts were Texans, but the most fitting description is "Okies".

The woman with the child remains a mystery to us. The baby was only two months old and yet the woman was noticeably pregnant.

At one small town the truck was halted in the middle of the wide main street and our friends disappeared into various stores without a word-while the town traffic went around the barrier! A liquor store caught our eyes and Dave and I bought a bottle of domestic port to be used for refreshment when the jolting ride was over.

Our next stop was under a tree in the middle of nowhere. Our hosts produced the result of their shopping and we were invited to a supper of hot dogs, baloney, cheese and bread. Again, may I remind the reader that "Those who have the least to share…"

Many times we would have abandoned the crude affair and sought a more comfortable form of transportation if it hadn't been for the fear of offending those who had been willing to share their lot.

It was 10:00 PM when we reached town and said thanks and goodbye to our hosts and walked away with a synthetic case of the D.T.'s from the rough ride.

As we had expected, all the hotels were filled and we were directed to the Lutheran Servicemen's Center. We were assigned to our bunks in the dorm, checked our overnight bag, and set out with our bottle of "vino" to get dinner and see the town. By the combination of having Spanish relatives and living in southern Calif. Dave speaks Spanish fairly well and knows his Mexican foods. At his suggestion we had a dinner of enchiladas enhanced by our "vino". Enchiladas consist of tiny cubes of meat in a hot-spiced sauce and covering several tortillas-sorts of unleavened, fried pancakes. The dinner was most satisfactory and put me in the mood to see the sights of the town.

The business district of San Antonio is nothing unusual, but the San Antonio River is unusual. Winding, snakelike thru the very heart of the city, it is clean, and entirely landscaped. Few places in the business district are far from the shaded benches that are spaced along the walks beside the narrow, canal-like river. It is truly a garden spot on its entire length. No well-planned city would go astray to copy such natural beauty in the heart of a stone city.

As the Service Center closes at 1:00 A.M. Sunday we retraced our steps and so to bed. Sunday we awoke to find a clear fine day awaiting our sightseeing pleasure. This morning we checked our friendly bottle of vino with our bag and went to breakfast.

Our first stop was the famed Alamo located in the very heart of town. We were quite surprised to find it was so well restored, since the old mission had been a ruin even before the historic battle of 1836.

The sights of the old mission and fort plus the museum of the Alamo occupied us for nearly three hours. At noon, in order to rest our tired feet we retired to a drugstore and wrote a few postcards while indulging in milkshakes.

We again wandered along the winding banks of the San Antonio River to take color pictures of the novel type park.

Our next undertaking was to travel by city bus to the outskirts and, after much confused wandering, locate another old Spanish Mission. The "Conception [sic] Mission" was the scene of a battle in 1835 and still stands in a well-preserved state. After long examination of the mission we realized that our time was growing short and we would have to begin our trek homeward.

Our bag was recovered from the Service Center checkroom and we treated ourselves to an Italian dinner again making use of our bottle of wine. We were even so reckless with time as to linger after our meal to drink wine and eat fresh rolls. "A loaf of bread, a jug of wine and thou." The quotation was timely and I seemed to strike a note of amusement in Dave when I remarked "Sometime I'll get a bottle of wine and a loaf of French bread-then Mer and I'll sit under a tree somewhere and I'll see if it's as good as it sounds."

A study of our map revealed a highway U.S. #281 that would reach Brownwood with only an added five miles to the way we had come south. We decided the change could only be for the better as traffic had been sparce coming down. After obtaining many conflicting and confusing directions we took a San Pedro St. bus to the outskirts of town and began our journey homeward.

Within the first hour we received three rides in nice cars, but all were short trips, although they did get us past the suburbs. The next was a ride offered by a little old woman driving alone. The ride was welcome, but after ten miles she turned into her road and we were again on a deserted highway in the middle of the vast nothingness that is Texas. Our stay at that crossroad was a long one. Cars passing were few and far between and a road sign showing 22 miles from San Antonio didn't help. We had left town at 3:30 P.M. and it was then 6:15 P.M. We had covered only 22 miles in 2 ½ hours and still had 165 miles to go. Would we reach camp by duty hours Monday A.M. or would we be stranded along the highway and A.W.O.L.? Many of the cars were filled and we could understand their passing us up. It's the cars with only one or two passengers and an empty back seat that hurt. Our faith in humanity reached a new low when two G.I.'s passed us up. Our uniforms were clean, we were clean shaven etc. so why? The bulk of the traffic was heading toward San Antonio and we had several offers of rides to town. One old rancher even stopped and offered a ride to town and a bottle of beer! It's the little things like that that keep up the faith in fellow humans. Between cars we carved on a huge cottonwood tree and seemed to have every prospect of cutting the darn thing down with our penknives! If only that farmer with the goats would come along! We'd be glad to have that ride at this stage! At 6:20 we decided that we'd wait until 6:30 P.M. and then cross the road and try to get back to San Antonio and get a bus to Brownwood. Five minutes later we got a ride, then another, then another. They were all short rides and at 8:30 P.M. we found ourselves in a tiny village called Blanco, Texas. Almost no traffic, growing dark; and still 150 miles from camp!

At 9:00 P.M. we got a ride with a lone Lt. going "up the road apiece." All Texans seem a bit close mouthed and this native son was a lawyer, which seemed to make him even more evasive. Maybe he just wanted an "out"-to get rid of us if he decided that he didn't like our company. He was really "a good Joe" and our only objection was that he passed up four other hitch-hiking G.I.'s that he could have carried. Maybe it was just his form of dry humor, but we traveled sixty miles and then stopped for coffee before he grinned and said he was going to Camp Bowie! We could have kissed him on the spot. We really rolled and made that 150 miles from Blanco in only three hours. Right into camp and there we were at only midnight.

We had only been out of camp 16 hours and had covered 376 miles and seen the sights of San Antonio.

We enjoyed ourselves and had spent very little yet decided that wartime hitch-hiking in Texas wasn't a good idea and "Quote the raven…."

Wed., 7.11.1945, Camp Bowie, Brownwood, Tex.
We've been checking over some of our new clothes, etc. We're getting all sorts of stuff. Plastic waterproof match boxes, a waterproof bag for clothes, and four rubber bags about 6"x12" for food. I also managed to get an extra one of those for the camera. The new sleeping bags seem pretty good. It's made of heavy olive-drab wool-like a heavy G.I. blanket and shaped like this [drawing like an exclamation point] with a hole for the head and a zipper down the front. Then there is a waterproof canvas cover of the same shape but without the zipper and having snap fasteners on the side. They sort of look like a mummy case.

I'm glad to hear that you had a good time at the shore over the weekend. You should be quite tan before long if you keep finding time for sunbaths now and then. Besides, I'm in favor of the sunbaths as you usually seem to write at the same time.

Thurs., 7.12.1945, Camp Bowie, Brownwood, Tex.
I see by the date that tomorrow will be Fri. the thirteenth, but that never did worry me very much and it's seemed like a good luck day since the Fri. 13th when we parked in front of "The Valley". It was that night that I decided not to put it off another day and to get your ring in the morning and you know the rest-in fact you also know the first part, but it remains that it was a Fri. 13th and held luck for both of us.

Today has been very, very, very hot and not a breath of air.

The finished film came this noon. I'll hold them for a day or two as a lot of the fellows want to see them. Then too we may be able to get a projector used for training film strips and see them on the screen. 15 of the 18 are pretty good. Got three good shots of the pillbox attack when we were using the flamethrower in Denver.

Speaking of Denver, we had a little demonstration to put on with mustard gas and Walt has a crop of blisters again! There was hardly enough of the gas to put a mask on for, and yet several places where Walt had had blisters at school puffed up again. It's queer how he reacts to that stuff. Still no news and advance party is still here. "*Here we sit like birds in the wilderness.*"

Sat., 7.14.1945, Camp Bowie, Brownwood, Tex.
"3/4 years of engaged bliss". A year or two ago if anyone had told me my engagement would run for 3/4 of a year before I married the girl of my choice, I'd have said it would never be that way…yet here we are, a starlit Saturday night, only nine months later and hundreds of miles apart.

So you were at one time really considering coming all the way down here! You had mentioned it but I never thought you really considered such a thing. Down here to the wilds of Texas with no chaperone, etc. You really must love me to ever consider that.

According to what we hear, our personal items to take will be limited to seven pounds. So now each man is going to put a package of soap, razor blades, toothpaste, etc. in a large box and then we'll crate it and ship it as part of the outfit's property. That way we'll be able to take about twice as much junk as usual. You'd swear I was going to open up a P.X. in China by the looks of all the soap, blades, toothpaste, films, lighter flints, etc. that I have stored in my locker.

Dearest, your education seems to have been neglected in things like melon and ice cream and ponchos. You know the bright colored blankets the Mexicans always seem to have slung over one shoulder? That is a poncho and is just like a blanket with a hole in the center and is worn like a cape. Those we have are of rubberized cloth, frustrating to make fit tight around the neck and have snap fasteners on the ends. They can also be used as a tent, 'tho we'll carry tents too.

It's a sad story about the watch strap. I haven't really gotten started onto it. Then too, I'm beginning to consider if I was smart after all as it seems overseas one of the greatest problems is mildew and rotting of leather. I'm thinking that even if I do find the strays I'll still take my metal band along just in case.

Tues., 7.17.1945, Camp Bowie, Brownwood, Tex.
We just saw the movie "Junior Miss'. When, where and with whom did I see the play. I'm sure I saw the play because I remembered the whole plot and everyone says it's a new movie. Maybe I saw it in Washington when I was at Fort Myer.

As you know we've been more or less laying around and swimming and playing ball, etc. Well an engineer outfit down the road has been teaching some of their men to run bulldozers. A few of us (eager beavers) bored with loafing got the OK to sit in on the bulldozer classes. As a result we were out in the hot sun all day without shirts. We can't learn to operate a bulldozer-that is grade roads, etc. in the time we'll have to play with them, but we can and have been able to learn to run the things and besides it's fun. I wouldn't want a job running one of the things, but the way I look at it a well-rounded education could be useful and it never hurts to learn anything from the classics to glorified ditch-digging. What's more the tractors drive just like a tank and someday I might save my neck by being able to drive a tank.

You are very sweet to send stamps, but from now on you'll be just as sweet and not need to send stamps. They've finally made an arrangement for our mail orderly to keep stamps on hand for sale to us. It's about time too because several of us were wondering about that business in China, Burma, or India.

I hear Hank Hatter is back from Africa and brought a dog back with him.

Wed., Thurs., 7.18.19.1945, Camp Bowie, Brownwood, Tex.
The current rumor is that we'll sail from either Portland, OR or Seattle, WA.

Thurs., 7.19.1945, Camp Bowie, Brownwood, Tex.
Dave Bush and I got a 3-day pass (Fri-Sun) to go to Dallas (Capt. said San Antonio is too far to go.) so we ended up getting

a 1 ½ day pass. We had planned to visit close friends of Mr. & Mrs. Cox then we were told there would be a weapon inspection in Bowie on Fri. morning so we requested Sat.-Mon. off. Then the inspection changed to Monday. Dave is still going, he's to meet his "Uncle" Robinson but doesn't know anyone in Dallas.

Sat., 7.21.1945, Camp Bowie, Tex. letterhead
Five of us were on an inspection team of weapons (for the Signal Corps outfit and Chemical Warfare outfit.)

We sunbathed and listened to a church service on the radio. I had to sew the seam on my swim trunks again.

Walt O'Connell had his wife Doris came to the camp for dinner.

Mon., 7.23.1945, Bowie, Brownwood, Tex.
Dave returned back to camp. He missed the bus so he hitchhiked and got a ride to Fort Worth.

I sent you a package and roses for your birthday and hope everything arrives on time.

Wed., 7.25.1945, Camp Bowie, Brownwood, Tex.
Today is your birthday. Many happy returns and I wish I could be there to kiss you. I wonder too if the dressing table set and roses arrived OK.

Please don't worry about the status of your bank account. The bonus is fine and all that, but for now we'll just be rich in love. Our feeling for each other makes us two of the richest people in the world.

We'll have retreat and rifle inspection in a few minutes and I'm showered and all dressed except for a shirt. I just finished a shower and now I'm a hot as ever. This heat is ROUGH!

After supper Dave Bush, another fellow, and I went swimming. After that we had our hearts set on milkshakes so we walked all the way to the service club only to find the soda bar closed. So we had to settle for Cokes and went to a movie. I told Dave

Bush that if I hang around him long enough I may be able to learn some Spanish and I'm teaching him French.

Thurs., 7.26.1945, Camp Bowie, Tex.
My parents got a letter from Geo. Jr. from the boat. He thinks he's headed for the Saipan area.

Dave and I are going out for enchiladas. I'm going to try to send you some of the recipes.

I keep thinking that I should have married you when I was home on furlough.

I've enclosed a picture of us shooting at radio-controlled target planes without pilots. We shoot from the back of the truck versus from turrets.

Sat., 7.28.1945, Camp Bowie, Brownwood, Tex.
Dave and I are able to swim almost nightly in the camp pool.
Fri., 8.3.1945, Camp Bowie, Brownwood, Tex.
Got the locks of your hair-now I'll have you even closer to me.

So, Eleanor [Stratton, later Bacon] got a ring, is that an engagement ring, and, if so, who's the lucky fellow?

Rumor has it that we'll be leaving Bowie on the 15th. The 471st company has the same orders we do and they're loading cases and crates on the train. They'll leave on the 10th and our group will follow on the 15th.

Tomorrow I'm finally going on my 3-day pass to Fort Worth (Fri., Sat., and Sun.) and Dave will meet me there on Saturday evening.

Sat., 8.4.1945, Fort Worth Service Men's Centers, Tex. letterhead
I finally got my laundry and left camp yesterday. Dave was to meet me here tonight, but as usual our plans went haywire. Our outfit had to furnish the alert guard for the weekend in case of riots, etc. so Dave couldn't even get the weekend off. I ended

up going to Fort Worth alone. I met a couple of our boys here and we spent the night drinking beer. I'm beginning to feel pretty much at home in this service center since I've been here so often.

We had German PW's here but the soldiers have been moved out and only the sailors remain.

Tues., 8.7.1945, Camp Bowie, Brownwood, Tex.
We had a party last night for the second platoon (30 of them). We got rye, hired a small tavern, and had a steak dinner. ($45 each).

This morning I had to guard for half the morning and also spent some time firing some rifles.

Dave and I discussed plans for his mountain "cabin". He's marrying into money and his future mother-in-law wants to build them a mountain cabin as a wedding present. Her version is more the size of a hotel versus his 3-4 room version. Hers is five bedrooms, five bathrooms, and two fireplaces!
I've mailed both you and my family a map and an explanation of how to interpret it using dollar signs for the distance. It shows both Okinawa and Pearl so that you'll be able to figure out where we're headed. The advance party left today and we expect to leave on the 15th. The trip to Seattle should take four days.

Bud wrote that he's expecting his discharge shortly.

This new atomic bomb business has us all on edge.

[Fragment, approximately **Mon., 8.6.1945**, U.S. Army, Camp Bowie, Brownwood, Tex.]
Yesterday I mailed a map to you and also a copy home. I mailed it by regular mail as it was a bit heavy for airmail. Here is what the idea is: You, my family, and I will each have a copy of the same map. I've changed the numbers on the map to fit my plan. Now, from now on, any of my letters that contain figures in the postscript only; those figures will refer to the map. The dollars will refer to the figures of the clocks on the map and the cents

will be fractions within the block. You'll always start to read the map from the lower left. The first amount I give will always be the distance from left to right. The second amount will always be the amount from bottom to top. It isn't nearly as hard as it sounds and you'll get it OK. Here's an example: P.S. remember that extra light I bought for $2.45 to take overseas? Well, we hadn't been on the boat two days before I sold it for $4.35. Big business deal! Love, Allen

When you look at the map you'll first look left to right to the #2 line and then 45% of the distance to #3. Then you'll read up on the map to the #4 line and 35% of the distance to the #5 line. When those two lines cross you'll find Okinawa. OK?

By the same system $6.10 and $4.10 would place me at Pearl. OK? I don't think you'll have any trouble after all you're a smart girl. You'd better not mention codes or maps after this as they may start to censor my mail any day now.
Oh, I didn't tell you yet did I? Our advance party left today and we expect to leave here on the 15th. The trip to Seattle will take four days and after that…?

Wed., 8.8.1945, U.S. Army, Camp Bowie, Brownwood, Tex.
First the atomic bomb and now Russia's help! I don't see how Japan can possibly hold out.

Our leaving date has been changed from August 15th to August 21st.

Don't know what happened to the slides that I sent to you. They seem to have gotten lost. I wonder if they were confiscated due to the photos I took of the plane and the school in Denver.

Thurs., 8.9.2015, U.S. Army, Camp Bowie, Brownwood, Tex.
Today we had a flash flood. Water started coming in and pretty soon we were sitting on the tables to keep dry. Busy day-I taught a two-hour refresher course on rifles and then a one-hour class on chemical warfare.

Sat., 8.11.1945, U.S. Army, Camp Bowie, Brownwood, Tex.
Yesterday we were expecting to hear that the peace had been made official. Now this morning it seems we refused the terms. In spite of it all, it's starting to look like the end of the war is in sight.

Dave and I are going to look for the town of San Angelo to the west of the camp for beer and to see the town.

We're due to leave Texas around the 21st and go to Seattle. Our neighbors, the 471st Truck Company has already left for Seattle.

Sun., 8.12.1945, U.S. Army, Camp Bowie, Brownwood, Tex., U.S.O. letterhead
We're at the U.S.O. in Brownwood and I think we've seen more of Texas than many Texans.

We spent the weekend in San Angelo was 105 miles from B'wood. It took us three legs of hitchhiking.

Now Dave's playing classical records here at the U.S.O.

We're all hoping that in the morning they'll announce VJ [Victory over Japan] Day.

Tues., 8.14.1945, Camp Bowie, Brownwood, Tex.
The peace is official! It will probably be a few more days 'tho until VJ Day but the peace seems sure now.

Three down and home to go! Now we can wonder what they'll have us doing between now and D-Day. D-Day means "Discharge Day".

We're expecting to leave on Monday. Our sister outfit, the 471st left on Saturday for Seattle but ended up in Ft. Bragg, N. Car.

I was just thinking, a month ago I was in Lake Charles daydreaming about an engagement ring and now I'm daydreaming about a wedding ring.

Darling, darling! It's all over! Truman just announced that it's all official!

It's been ten months [correct?] since we got engaged and now I'm hoping to become a civilian and then a husband. Speaking of wedding rings and things- Dave and I were talking and he said his girl talked him into a double ring job. I know you and I disagree on the double rings and our first kiss.

Wed., 8.15.1945, Camp Bowie, Brownwood, Tex.
We drove some tanks over to the other side of the camp. The radio announced that gasoline rationing is at an end right now.

Somehow, I don't think the Army is ready to let go of me yet. I have no overseas service, very few points, and I'm not married. I bet that George, Jr. feels he's getting his overseas duty at just the wrong time.

You asked-Clyde is in the first platoon and Walt is in the third platoon.

Thurs., 8.16.1945, Camp Bowie, Brownwood, Tex.
We are still planning to leave Bowie on Tuesday. I should be due for a furlough sometime in the middle of September.

Fri., 8.17.1945, Camp Bowie, Brownwood, Tex.
We swim in the pool almost every day. Friday is the day we put our beds out to air.

Sat., 8.18.1945, Camp Bowie, Brownwood, Tex.
I've mailed a company plate to you.

Sun., 8.19.1945, Camp Bowie, Brownwood, Tex.
We're still scheduled to leave on Tuesday. All our things that we want or need for the five-day trip will get carried in our field bags (including cameras and film). We're also taking developing chemicals and some equipment that we purchased out of the company fund. We'll wear fatigue uniforms on the train. We're hoping for AC Pullman cars instead of the troop sleepers.

Dave has finished high school and has one year of junior college. He'll be 21 next month. He plays the clarinet and has done some symphony work.

It was 106 degrees yesterday.

Mon., 8.20.1945, Camp Bowie, Brownwood, Tex.
It feels like the war is finally over and we have hopes that our outfit will be broken up.

Wed., 8.22.1945, traveling by train to Seattle
We're in an old but comfortable non-AC Pullman. We've passed Syracuse, Kan. but we're not taking the route that we used to go to Denver before. Got to Denver at night. Walt's family met us at the station. We were scheduled to be here for only 10 minutes but that turned into two hours. We've passed Rawlings, Wyo. and are headed towards Salt Lake City.

Thurs., 8.23.1945, traveling by train to Seattle
We are in Rock Springs, Wyo. by way of Fort Worth, Oklahoma City, Wichita, Kans., Pueblo, Col., Denver, Col., and Rawlins, Wyo. We spend most of our time playing cribbage. We've seen Pikes Peak and are traveling in a long troop train in a Pullman car. Now we're headed for Salt Lake City.

Fri., 8.24.1945, traveling by train to Seattle
Still traveling. We have gotten to Pocatello, Idaho

[Undated postcard]
Didn't stop in Salt Lake City. Spent most of our time playing cribbage. I just learned to play it the day before yesterday.

Sat., 8.25.1945, location unknown
Well, we've finally arrived here 'tho I can't tell you where "here" is. We did come to the place we thought we would, but only stayed a few hours and then came here. Yes, as you can see the censorship of mail is still on so I can't tell you much. In fact, we don't know much except that we all expect to be seasick before too long.

The trip was more a vacation than a hardship. We had regular Pullmans instead of troop sleepers and got here this afternoon. Most of the trip was cool enough that we kept the window closed and here it's so cool that we've put on our wool uniforms.

CHAPTER 5
Camp Lewis, Takoma, Washington And Fort Lawton, Seattle, Washington

Mon., 8.27.1945, Camp Lewis, Tacoma, Wash.
My last letter was returned because I wasn't allowed to write about our train route. We didn't go to Salt Lake City but ended up following the Columbia River across Oregon. We arrived at Fort Lawton in Seattle, unpacked for five hours, and there were ordered to Fort Lewis just outside Tacoma (61 mi.) by truck. Tomorrow we're moving back to Fort Lawton again. Dave and I are working on making a leather cribbage board that can be rolled up and carried in our pocket.

Tues., 8.28.1945, Fort Lawton, Seattle, Wash.
[Sent her his APO address. Letter heavily censored]
Dave and I spent time trying to find material to make a cribbage board.

Wed., 8.29.1945, Fort Lawton, Seattle, Wash.
We're sailing tomorrow. Dave and I spent the night in Seattle. We're back at Fort Lawton now.

Thurs., 8.30.1945, Fort Lawton, Seattle, Wash.
Today we're going back to where we were supposed to go in the first place. I've sent home the leather film case that you made for me.

George's APO has changed and he has finally landed.

Tried "bolling [sic] on the green" with weighted balls.

So, you're contemplating leaving Dr. Herman [Nathan B. Herman, M.D., Mer's boss] because of the amount of work. You know what is best for you.

I do have Odie's [Frank Odenheimer] number in my book. Bud and Jane owe me a letter.

I think once we head overseas the worst that can happen will be seasickness.

CHAPTER 6

At Sea on the *U.S.S. George W. Julian*

Fri., 8.31.1945, at sea
It's very crowded onboard. We don't know for sure where we are going yet.

Fri., 9.7.1945, at sea
At sea. Our newscasts say that censorship has been lifted. We're stopping at Pearl tomorrow. Dave is hoping to go ashore tomorrow so he can see his birthplace although he left when he was very young. We left Seattle on Thurs. August 30th on a 200-foot Army transport, the *S.S. George W. Julian*. We have air corps men along on the trip as well. The ship serves three meals a day and the PX has Watermen pens ($8 for 4). Our ship was to go to Saipan but was cancelled once we were at sea and we were told to stage at Pearl instead. We should be getting there tomorrow. Our ship is alone without even a convoy. So far, we've only seen three ships and they were at a distance. The Red Cross supplied us with cards to fill the time. The night before last the blackout was lifted. Our ship's public address system plays jazz, classical music, news, and shortwave Bob Hope programs. Morale is low because other fellows are going home already.

Dave Bush left this area when he was one year old.
There is a 5 ½ hour time difference here.

I'm growing a Van Dyke beard.

Sun., 9.9.1945, Pearl Harbor, Honolulu, HI
We had some storms and part of the truck cargo broke loose and knocked a hole in the ship. It has taken us nine days to reach Pearl. We left on August 30th and got here yesterday. We went thru Kauai Strait and halfway circled Oahu. The only evidence we've seen so far of Dec. 7th was one battered hulk and one wrecked airplane.

We were supposed to go to Saipan but our orders were changed in the middle of the ocean. We are not allowed off our ship (the *George W. Julian*, a liberty ship built in 1943, approx.. 250 ft. with 1,088 troops aboard). We've been able to see Honolulu and Waikiki Beach and the Royal Hawaiian Hotel. The military has a huge installation at Pearl with ships, planes, carriers, and dry-docks. Our ship is tied up rail to rail with many cargo ships due to the limited number of piers. We expect to leave tomorrow.

Tues., 9.11.1945, Pearl Harbor, Honolulu, HI and at sea
We didn't leave Pearl yesterday. Got a chance to look around some more. There are hills and everything is a vivid green. There is a blue sky but dark clouds over the hills and we get light showers for a minute or two about every 10 minutes resulting in a large number of rainbows.

We watched the huge ship *Saratoga* leave yesterday with 3,800 men to be discharged.

We have left Pearl and are going to Saipan. No convoy again. Saipan is supposed to be 10-12 days away.

Wed., 9.12.1945, at sea
Our fresh water is being rationed except at drinking fountains. Salt water is used for all our showers and for washing clothes. The way clothes are washed is to tie a rope to the clothes and drag them in the ocean for a few hours. Had our second Atabrine pill. We are getting one Coke per person tomorrow.

Thurs., 9.13.1945, at sea
Our destination is still Saipan but we may stop in Enewetak [Marshall Islands]. We're expecting our ship to cross the International Date Line today. We saw a B-29 overhead yesterday. They're still feeding the 470th Atabrine each day and we seem to be the only outfit to get it. (It doesn't prevent malaria but calms the symptoms.)

About half our unit has over 45 points already and should never have even left the States. There are about ten men with 60-70 points and about ten men who are over 38 years old.

Mon., 9.17.1945, at sea
Hundreds of the men are sleeping up on the decks. Our censorship has been taken off but they still haven't returned our cameras to us yet. We're getting to Enewetak Atoll tomorrow to refuel.

Refueling station is one mile round and six feet high. We don't expect to stay in Saipan for very long. Saipan is reported to have an ice cream plant and a Coke bottling plant. Mostly it is an air base. They shouldn't have much use for a truck outfit since the island is only 14 miles long and four miles wide.

We hear there is a bill being introduced to discharge men with 72 pts. service.

I've cut my sideburns but still have the moustache and the Van Dyke. I may have to shave the beard before leaving the ship 'tho. There are 1,088 of us onboard ship and there has not been a single fight.

We arrived at Saipan last night after leaving Enewetak on the western edge of the Marshall Islands and listed as Brown Atoll. The Captain said no cameras will be used aboard the ship.

You ask about our wedding music. I have no suggestions for you.

I am hoping to write to George and get his location. George talked about natives as Micronesians so he's probably somewhere in the area of the Mariana Island (Saipan), Marshall Islands (Enewetak) or the Caroline Islands.

It costs six cents per ½ oz. for airmail and there is a shortage of stamps onboard the ship.

There were many ships at the atoll- submarines, carriers, battleships, cargo ships, hospital ships, tankers, troop ships, etc. Large seaplanes as well and there must be a landing strip due to the number of planes we are seeing. Newscasts are saying that they are using aircraft carriers as extra transports. If the West Coast railroads get too crowded with returning troops they may end up taking some of the troops through the Panama Canal to the East Coast.

News is by late winter the Army will abandon the point system and men with two years' service will be released!

Wed., 9.19.1945, at sea
Many onboard have grown beards.

Fri., 9.21.1945 V-mail, Enewetak Atoll
Just a small note. I'm dropping this off at the atoll where we stopped. Airmail is uncertain until we get to Saipan in about five days.

Sat., 9.22.1945, at sea
Twenty-three days onboard ship without getting off. We are at sea again and should reach Saipan on Tuesday or Wednesday. We had to pull all of our clothes out of our duffle bags to be sprayed with insect repellant. Ours seemed to be the only one that had to do that.

We are now getting fresh water for three hours per day but showers, shaving and washing is still done with saltwater and we even have saltwater soap.

Mon., 9.24.1945, at sea
We got one Coke per man today- the second of the trip. We play cribbage a lot to pass the time. The only work we have done so far on the trip was to clean five rifles belonging to the ship.

My best piece of clothing that I have brought so far has been my moccasins. Many men only brought their combat boots and they are heavy and hot in this climate.

They returned our cameras to us today. I am taking some pictures onboard and will probably send them to you to have two prints developed for the fellows.

CHAPTER 7
Saipan

Wed., 9.26.1945, Saipan
Dave and I were just checking up and we decided that I'm only between eight and nine thousand miles from home.

When we got up yesterday (the 25th) there were two islands in sight and until lunch we had a lot of discussion as to which was Saipan and which was Tinian. (They are only about a mile apart.) Tinian is the smaller of the two and a flat, high plateau. Finally at about 4:00 PM we tied up to a pier and landed on Saipan. It's very green, a good number of trees, and hilly with a few cliffs. After much lugging around of heavy duffle bags, field bags, gas masks, rifles, etc. we ended up at our tents and went right to chow. As soon as we walked out of the mess hall our mail was handed to us! I had 17 waiting for me!

The setup looks very much better than we expected. It's just about like being in garrison in the States. Right now we're living in large six-man tents with a wood frame and wood floors. We sleep on folding canvas cots. We don't have any lights, but the rest of the island has electric lights, radios, etc. There's even a regular radio station on the island and small daily paper. In a few days another outfit will move out and we will move into plywood barracks. They are one-story Pacific Huts with screens, lights, cots, and even some have a mattress on the cot. Malaria seems at a low rate and we haven't been given Atabrine for the past two days although we put our nets up over our bunks.

The natives live about four miles away and about a mile away are two large Marine cemeteries. There is an Army cemetery and B-29 installations about ten miles away. We are very close to Guam. There are Jap. prisoners.

As yet we don't know what Army we're under 'tho rumor says that we're under the First. Div. and under Pearl Harbor command. We're not sure what our work will be but it seems we'll drive trucks that load and unload ships. We're no longer under the 4th Army. The 4th in Texas and the 2nd in Tenn. seem to be mainly stateside training armies like the 1st, 2nd, 3rd, and 4th. Air Forces are for the Air Corps. The shoulder patch is something like blue background, diagonal arrow in red and white stars above and below the arrow. But patches are for dress clothes and I doubt if we'll have any use for dress clothes here.

There's a swimming beach about nine miles up the beach and we're eager to get to that. My trunks fell apart on the ship and I had to buy a pair at sea. I would say please send me swimming trunks for Christmas, but by the time I got them I will have ripped off some suntans or fashioned something.

So far the food seems pretty good- it's almost all dehydrated and all canned, but lots of jams, jellies, and even large cans of hard candy on the table. At breakfast I even had almost a quart of ice-cold grapefruit juice. The P.X. sell cans of all fruit juices and lots of brands of gum and candy that I haven't seen for a long, long time.

One thing you might try sending once every week or two would be the back page (Balto. Topics) of *The Sun.*, *The Evening Sun* would be OK as your dad takes the morning paper.

Beer is rationed to six bottles per man per week. There are lots of mosquitoes and we have nets over our beds.

Thurs., 9.27.1945, Saipan
There are three platoons working in eight-hour shifts. There are still a few hundred Japs in the hills who don't know that the war is over, but don't cause much trouble although a naval officer was killed last week while looking for souvenirs. The PX has Cokes about four days a week.

It rains for 10-15 minutes two or three times a day without warning. There are gravity flow showers with walls and cement floors but no roof.

The washstands are entirely open air and just against the outside wall of the shower room. So far, we eat out of mess kits, but they say trays will be issued. Each man washes his own tray, etc. and keeps it in his tent. There is a washing machine for clothes but we haven't had to try to get to see if it works.

I haven't seen any woman, white or black, since we left the States.

There are hundreds of Jap PW's [Prisoners of War] confined and running loose working here and there are supposedly Jap native women but we haven't seen any of them yet.

So, you caught the bouquet at Weesie's [Louise Zimmerman, Mer's cousin] wedding. I hope that proves to be a good omen.

The family tells me that one word was censored from one letter from Seattle when I mentioned pictures. The censored part was "totem poles" as Dave and I took pictures of one in Seattle.

Men who are returning from overseas are now getting 30-45-day furloughs. We may consider combining our nest egg to buy a car when I get back, get married, and take a Mexican honeymoon while I'm on my furlough. Once I start working, vacations are usually two weeks and that won't be long enough for Mexico and our trip might end up as one of those things we always wanted to do.

Fri., 9.28.1945, Saipan
We are supervising the unloading of ships. The ships were slated for the Japanese invasion and all their trucks have a smokestack-like an exhaust pipe sticking up in the air from the hood. Very loud.

Take my film to Ritz, Stark, or somewhere and have just strips of small contact prints made for me.

I am writing this by candlelight.

Sat., 9.29.1945, Saipan
Bush hauls bread around so he can pilfer food easily. We are able to wear any type clothes we want.

Rumor has it there is a proposal to let men out after two years' service or even three years' service.

Mon., 10.1.1945, Saipan
This is supposed to be the end of the rainy season- was raining 4-5 times a day. Everything is soggy-writing cases, tobacco pouches; envelopes stick in spite of waxing the flaps. If this is life in the tropics take me back to the States. 14 of our men are starting the processing to go home. The 10th Army is going to return to the States and then disband- Odie should be getting to stateside soon. We got to go swimming on a sandy beach with nice bottom sand and the water is clear. The breakers are almost ½ mile out so you can really swim near the beach. The water is chest deep for about two blocks from shore. There is a diving platform that is a diving board on top of a wrecked Sherman tank. Hundreds of GI's are swimming off tiny speedboats and sailboats-almost all made of streamlined airplane fuel tanks and are only about five feet long. Some are single tank, tank with an outrigger, or two tanks. The motors are rebuilt air compressor motors and are either built in the boat or on the ones with two tanks the motor is in the center. Dave and I may try to build a sailboat.

Mud is everywhere and I can only wear my moccasins indoors. The Gooks are all the natives- Koreans, Hawaiians, Arabs or what have you. In this case they're Korean laborers.

I want the sun to come out so that I can get pictures of the Gook shacks, Jap caves, the island, etc.

They are dropping surrender leaflets on the Japs. George and Odie are both in Okinawa.

Dave and I are having midnight snacks of K-rations. There are enough there to last for years- whole fields stacked ten feet high. Last night we finished the first case (12 breakfast units, 12 dinners, and 12 suppers). We heat the coffee; eat cheese and crackers, chocolate bars, chewing gum, hash, cigarettes, fruit bars, etc. The darn things even provide us with matches! Rough war!

The pictures I've taken so far included Bowie, the train stops, cliff at Green River [in Wyo., Utah, Col.] the Columbia River, Takoma, Dave with his moustache/Van Dyke and yours truly. There are a few shots of the boys on deck, distant shots of Tinian and Saipan and me and Dave with moustaches alone. One shows Leon, James, Clarence Johnson (blond with wonderful build) and Dave and one with others and me that Dave took with the background of banana trees. I'm not used to the black and white film.

I wonder what your reaction is to my idea about getting married and going to Mexico while I'm on my furlough. Under the G.I. Bill if I can't get a job and work while I'm going to school the government will still pay me $50.00 per month and $75.00 if married.

Some Joe offered to trade Dave a motor scooter for his folding camera. At that rate I should be able to get a sedan for mine.

I made shorts out of a pair of pants, hemmed them, cut the patch pocket off, put a hip pocket in and a zipper pocket in front. I even cut the belt loops off and put a short belt on the front.

Dave didn't get up for breakfast and is heating his K-ration of chopped ham and eggs over a candle.

Our movies are outdoors and we wear ponchos in case of the usual showers. One Lt. grabbed his poncho and found he'd grabbed his waterproof clothing bag (like a barrack bag).

I ate half of Dave's cereal, some sort of bran with powdered milk and sugar added. You eat it raw or with water.

It's payday but what good is money here. I'm sending home $25.00 a month and wondering how much life insurance I should carry. I'm not sure if I should hold my Army insurance and convert it to civilian insurance or convert part of it or let it drop. I have $6,000 in civilian policy now without the $10,000 of Army insurance.

Dave wrote and sealed a letter this morning and the dampness has caused the envelope to just fall apart. If we stay here long enough I guess we'll just get fat and get webbed feet.

We have a gasoline lantern now. The six of us in our tent are the only ones who haven't moved to the barracks yet.

Tues., 10.2.1945, Saipan
Rain and mud. Can't think of anything for Christmas that would be of use and wouldn't get in the way. I would like a good tobacco humidor with a pipe rack once I get home.

A Gook stuck his head in the tent and started to jabber. We didn't understand him and then found out he was selling rag dolls the Korean women made for $2.00 with black hair piled on top and in native dress.

Some of the boys have been exploring Jap. areas but all they find are bullets, grenades, bayonets, etc. Then too, they always run the risk of a dud or a booby-trap so it's best not to fool around with the stuff. There are still Japs up in the mountains refusing to believe the war is over.
Dave finished a snack of pork loaf mixed with breadcrumbs that I whipped up and cooked over our stove (a can filled with sand and soaked with gasoline-quite safe). We are eating well.

Both of us seem to be in favor of "Ave Maria" and "Libestraum". I can't recall "Meditation" but Dave thinks it would go well.

Don't worry about saving. We get overseas pay and there is no place to spend money and I never play cards or cribbage for money.

I'm the only one in the tent with a picture up. Even Dave didn't bring a large picture of Nan (his betrothed). And two of the fellows are married too! Tsk. Tsk.

Dave and I routinely swim at the beach. There aren't any waves.

We've shifted the beds to the middle of the tent to escape the leaks. Most of the fellows are in tents except our group of six.

Fri., 10.5.1945, Saipan
Rain and heavy winds and we thought that our tent would blow over. We're told that this flow is the typhoon that'll hit us in 24-48 hours. We tied the tent down and put plywood around the sides. Around here we do well to keep only soaked to the skin all the time. Everything we own is wet, soggy or damp. They may as well cut the ropes or whatever is holding it and let the damn island sink.

I have a steady job now. Leave it to "Naussberg"! I'm in the rubber tire business. One other Joe and I run the tire repair shop for the whole island but the funny part is we never touch a tire! We have 20 Gooks to do the work and we supervise. They know their job so well that all we have to do is sit around and tell the "number one boy" what we want done. If they start to loaf all we do is yell "Chop, chop!" and they scramble back to work. Maybe I'll jabber in Korean when I get back. They're good-natured and good workers and seem quite willing to accept us as "boss man". A truck driver comes in with a flat and removes the wheel from the truck. He takes a good tire and wheel from our supply and puts that on his truck in place of the flat. I sign his trip ticket with the time he arrived and the time he left to show where he was and then he leaves. Our Gooks pounce on the flat tire, repair it, and put it on the wheel and stand it aside for the next man who comes in. We, or rather they, repair 50-60 flats a day. In their spare time they squat on their heels and talk or play games. I'll never understand how they can be comfortable squatting like that, but they seem to prefer it to a chair! Their main game seems to be something like jacks only played with little rocks. They toss one in the air and see how many they can pick up and still catch the first one. Our directions to them are limited to "Hey!", "OK", "Chop-Chop" and pointing but they can speak one or two words of English-which is better than we do in Korean! But then they want to learn English because they want to come to the States but no G.I. wants to learn Korean because no G.I. wants to go to Korea. You know I've always thought I'd like to be able to sit around and yell "Chop-Chop" at a Chinese or Jap houseboy but I never thought I'd be doing it for 20 of them! The Army pays them 50 cents a day plus their meals and that's a fairly good wage for them. You should see how they live! If the rain ever stops maybe I'll be able to get pictures of the shacks. The ones who farm a little plot of land for food do their plowing with oxen! At least they seem to keep clean, most clean clothes and always seem to be washing their faces and hands.

We drove up to the far end of the island and passed something we didn't know existed "U.S. Gov't Leper Colony Keep Out!" Don't worry, we did- and will! We kept right on driving! The enclosures are just a safe conduct pass and some other of our propaganda.

Sun., 10.7.1945, Saipan
We just heard that men in the States with two years' service are starting to get discharges and that makes me feel sorry for myself. But still more power to those boys if they can get out. Just because we're stuck here due to lack of transportation there's no reason they should be forced to stay in the Army too. The only point is that it was never necessary for us to leave the States in the first place. Oh well, someday…

The folks just forwarded George's first uncensored letter and Enewetak was their first stop. They didn't put in at Pearl. He also expected to be leaving Okinawa soon and going to Japan.

The typhoon we were expecting went around and missed us.

If my life with all these Gooks keeps up I don't think I'll come back speaking Korean, but there is a real danger I'll be using a lot of basic English like "You come" "You tire fix, and "Time go lunch".

Today I got Dave to take a picture of us before and (just had to fill my pen and at this rate in another week the cap of Dave's ink will rust all the way thru) at any rate, he took pictures of me wearing a suit of fatigues and then wearing those I cut up. I cut the pants into shorts-deluxe jobs with built-in belt, zipper, pocket, hip pockets, etc. The jacket I cut into a waist length mess-jacket with short sleeves. I'm becoming quite a seamstress.
We're still the lone Indians living in tents and we like it here. There's room in the barracks now, but we'll stay here until we're forced to move.

We've been to the movies quite a bit but haven't seen anything exceptional that I hadn't seen before.

We still eat midnight snacks of K-rations and play a lot of cribbage. In fact, we built a cribbage board into our table-top and since we eat cheese and crackers so often Dave put a sign on the table: "Please do not clog cribbage holes with cheese!" Just finished drinking two cold cans of good "Mt. Ranier" (Seattle) beer and it was easy to drink.

I got a picture today of "Suicide Cliff". That's the one so many Japs jumped from rather than be captured and it's only about 100 yards behind our tents. (We're at the bottom-don't worry.)

Dave broke the mainspring of his watch the first day we hit the island. It's little things like that that make us realize how far we are from civilization.

We're getting quite a little home here in the tent. At first we had darkness, then it was candles, then a gasoline lantern.

Now we have two gasoline lanterns, tables, chairs, etc. If we're here much longer we'll run wires and put in electric lights.

I've always liked everything towards the "Valley" but even 'tho trains are OK for business you must remember that I expect to be going to school in the center of town almost every evening. So on that score maybe get an apartment in town would be the best setup first for us. I think you are right about it's being a good idea to arrange it that your rent buys your home and you're also right about wanting to buy a more individualized home.

Dave is across the table pulling envelopes and stamps apart. That is a never-ending problem. We've put wax on them, hair oil, powder, etc. and still they stick until you want them to stick.

So, you're getting fat! A fine thing! Please at least keep below Mrs. _____ so I can at least get my arms around you.

Tues., 10.9.1945, Saipan
It's only raining about three or four times a day now.

Yesterday we moved into the barracks. It's better in some ways-mattress, electric lights, etc. but it seems more crowded and some fellows drive at night so we hear them come in at night. Dave and I spent almost two hours sawing plywood for two lockers for our clothes. They are all cut out now and maybe we'll find time tomorrow to put them together. I hate to go to work so early in the morning (5:45 AM) but getting off at 2:00 PM has its points. Dave is usually off by 1:00 PM so after we get our stuff set up we should be able to swim once and awhile in afternoons. Did I tell you Dave is the bread and ration man for the outfit? He drives a truck to the bakery every morning and gets the bread. Once a week he also gets all the canned goods, etc. Speaking of food, today we had fresh oranges and baked potatoes- not dehydrated potatoes, but real potatoes.

The reason that I have to start to work so early is that I have to drive a truck clear up to the other end of the island to pick up our Gooks. They live in a big wire-enclosed cage with their wives and families. A labor officer checks them as they come out of the gate and then I have to sign for them. It's really funny-every last one of them grins and says "Good morning" as he comes out and I have to say to 48 of them one at a time! Only 28 of them work for me in the tire shop and the others work in other places in the motor pool. It's sort of a shock to realize that their English vocabulary is so limited and yet 50% of the words they know are profane or obscene. They are nice 'tho and easy to get along with. They're willing to work hard, but we sure don't! We're told not to work while we're with them because then they'll lose their respect for us. Our greatest worries are by no means about the tires- that part always seems to go smoothly. Yesterday our trouble was soap! They came to us and told us it was time to get soap. I asked "number one boy" if he "know where get soap?" He nodded so I took him along in the truck. When we got out on the road, I said "Which way?" and he didn't seem to understand. I didn't know what to do so I went up to our supply room and got five bars of G.I. soap. When he saw that he seemed a bit disturbed and jabbered a lot. What a row when we got back with that soap! Finally, they located some other different "number one boy" who spoke pretty good English and he explained that the natives get a ration of one bar per man every week and they get the soap once a month! We took the matter up with battalion supply and they claimed it was two bars per man per month. However, we got a full case (60 bars) and took it to them. Again, there was much jabbering and counting of bars so we told them to use that and we'd get them some more! There's probably enough soap (like everything else) on this island to sink a ship. When you get gasoline here all you do is stop at a pump, fill your tank and drive away. There is nothing to sign or anyone to ask…just take what you can use.

There is 14 hours difference between us now that you're off war time.

We're working on a sailboat in our free time.

We found a darkroom and may see what we can do with it.

Bush hopes to be out of the Army by April.

Fri., 10.12.1945, Saipan
I have three or four Gooks reading this over my shoulder but it is OK because they can only read one word here and there and with my penmanship they'll do well to do that. The other day I helped one or two with their attempt to read and write English and now I'm a tutor most of the time. They pick it up fairly fast and it's like teaching first or second grade. Almost all of them already know the alphabet so that is a start. A few can write simple sentences like "What time is it." "Where is your home." etc. "Gwahn Suhng Ohk"-that's the name of our "number one boy". Gawd knows how you say it! I've just been explaining to him about periods, question marks, and capital letters. He's having a bit of trouble as to when to use a question mark, but otherwise OK. He just pointed to my pen and asked me to show him how to write "ink" or as he says "inker". Yesterday I got a reward for my troubles-one fellow painstakingly wrote "I like you" and grinned. I'll probably tell them "If you ever get to the States-look me up." Then maybe we'll come home some night and find a circle of little brown men squatting on the floor.

I got a letter from home and it was the first I've heard that they've received my first letter from Saipan. That first letter was dated September 25th postmarked September 26th and they got it October 3rd.

We have a photo darkroom set up now and are starting to develop and print some film. I should be able to get copies of some of the prints, so since I have a lot of film I may sell my black and white film and take all my pictures in color and get copies of their black and whites.

The Gooks clothing is cast-off G.I., Navy and Marine plus whatever they "pick up". It seems strange to see a native wearing a shirt with "Cohen" or "Smith" on the back.

I believe that ponchos are the best designed and most useful thing the Army issues. Talk about the Londoners and their umbrellas, on Saipan it is the G.I. and his poncho. Most of us are now in the habit of keeping our ponchos with us at all times-no matter how bright the sun or how clear the sky. It rains at the most unexpected times and really pours. Then it will stop as suddenly as it began-as 'tho someone shut the water off!

Now they're going to let us take our sweaters, wool sleeping bags, and stuff like that into supply so we'll have a little less junk to take care of. Yesterday I spent a lot of time putting up a light at the head of my bed so I can read in bed and today they decided to move us around so that even working at night won't be disturbing the men who work during the day. So I'll have to tear it down and put it up someplace else-this is still the Army. Now we have to walk almost a block to wash and shower. Trucks with tanks haul water to the showers and pump the fresh water into a big tank on top of each shower. Yesterday the truck backed into our tent and knocked the whole d--- thing over. So, we have to use another shower for about a week until they can get ours fixed.
A whole year- and I used to think I favored fairly long engagements, but this is too long. I wish I could get home and end our engagement and you know how I'd like to end it. The radio announced yesterday that men with two years' service will be up for discharge about March 20th. We all hope that that means men with three years will be out by then.

Most of the natives have been here around three years and came with the Japs as conscripted labor and would like to go home as much as we would.

Dad said to try to have a color photo taken of myself to see if the suntan and Atabrine yellow show up. I thought I mentioned that we stopped taking Atabrine when we got off the boat and I've lost most of my tan since we stay out of the sun as much as possible.

I'd be willing to bet everything that we'll be married before another October 14th rolls around. Just heard that Katira Agnew (McCall)'s husband in the Army was killed and he has a child he never saw.

Sun., 10.14.1945, Saipan
"Our Day" This is the time and date that we were first engaged. Let's hope by this time next year we'll be well on our way towards our first wedding anniversary.

I finished the first color film yesterday but I'm sorry to say it'll be quite a while before you see them. After much thought I sent it to Eastman by air and enclosed stamps for the slides to be returned by air. Then I'll send them to you in letters.

We're getting pretty well settled now with barracks, reading light over my bed. I made a rubber air-pillow and I even made a pair of gook-type clogs for the shower. They're really comfortable too!

Yesterday I had to take two of our Gooks up to the native hospital. One for a small cut and the other to have a tooth pulled. These trips into the native camp enclosure are a good chance to observe them. I'm even beginning to be able to tell which are Japs, Koreans and Camorras (those speak a sort of Spanish). I still have hopes of getting pictures of things like ox-carts, etc. but it's too bad photos aren't allowed inside the native camp. I saw hundreds of little children in classes, playing, and planting a garden. The floors of their homes are as spotless as anything you ever saw because they never wear shoes inside and always sit on the floor. Most of the men wear G.I. clothes and shoes but women and children still go barefoot or wear clogs. Children under five years are bare period. Boys have short haircuts and the little girls wear a sort of Chinese bob. The older girls wear it gathered on each side and fairly long. Most of the women pull it straight back and a bun in back. I haven't seen any with the old type of piled-up hairdo.

Today Dave and I and another fellow took a tour of the island (46 mi.) and got a lot of pictures including one of my crew of Gooks. Most of our pictures were of roadside billboards showing pretty girls and a verse about care of tires or driving fast, etc. they are quite good and should be great in color.

May our engagement never see another anniversary.

Tues., 10.16.1945, Saipan
Dave and I ended up taking a gook to the gook hospital at the end of the island.

I'm not having Eastman send the second color film to you either. The mail clerk thought my return address should be with the film and there wasn't enough room for yours, mine and Eastman's. I corrected a mistake I made on the last one and I sent this one to Los Angeles to be developed. Whenever I get another ready I think I'll send it to Australia to be done. Eastman develops them there and that would be only one day by air.

The radio is still giving reports about all the damage on Okinawa and says many are shelter-less. I hope Geo. and Odie made it out OK.

The rainy season here seems to have tapered off and now we only have the usual showers.

I wonder if my mother got my letter in time and understood to send you roses for the 14th.

Just think 18 cents for a two-day flight to the States or one-day flight to Australia, just because it's to a different country.

I found out that yours truly finally made Cpl. Now I'm sure the war is over when this outfit agrees to throw another stripe my way. That'll give me $66 a month instead of $54 and my overseas pay and then too next month I start getting another 5% for 3-years' service.

Bush and I are drinking two cans of beer apiece in honor of my stripe and he saw me address my letter and a discussion followed. Verbal remarks refer to "Cpl." But the rating "5" is really "T/5" or Technician 5th Grade- but don't worry- the pay is the same as straight Cpl.

That idea of yours about my Christmas gift being toward the Mexican honeymoon is the best Christmas gift I've heard of yet. I've only got one suggestion to make on the idea. Don't send it to me. Keep it or deposit it or something because it isn't a good idea to keep much cash here. I take it you're planning on an evening wedding and my tails will be proper (if I can still wear them)- or were you thinking of a morning job? We've never discussed that have we? I have tails, but I don't have formal morning dress.

Dave just finished his letter and remarked "the folks will think times are rough!" He used all sorts of paper (as I have) then spilled beer on the letter; then the envelope was stuck and he had to open it and seal it with the clear nail polish that I keep for varied jobs like sealing watch crystal, cribbage boards, etc.

Around here we never know what we'll see (movies) til the picture starts. It's a strange setup, but if they listed the shows then some places would be jammed and others barren. They change shows every day, so where we go we just take a chance.

Mail home from Pearl left here today with another load of discharge-happy boys. I noticed that you write about "application" for discharge. That isn't the way it is. The Army seems to assume you want out and when your chance comes the papers start to go through unless you "apply" to stay in. Got it?

OK, civilian clothes for furlough wedding. I'd rather wear "civies" too. I don't know how the Army stands on that now or how things will be then, but if it came to that I'd just "assume" civies were OK and wear them. Then if there were any objection I'd say "I'm sorry, pardon my ignorance but what's done is done." That's the way life is over here. You just go ahead and do what you think is right; then if anyone objects you worry who was right.

Magazines! I know you want to send me things dearest, but there seems nothing I need. We get overseas editions (poorly sized, without ads) of *Life, Readers Digest, Look*, etc. and even *New Yorker*! Besides that we don't buy them- they're issued to each outfit.

Did I tell you one of our boys bought a monkey? Now don't ask me what on earth he's going to do with the critter! I haven't the slightest idea and neither does he. Some people have more dollars than sense. (The critter cost twenty bucks!) Right now he's (the monkey, 'tho it should be the owner) is living in a large cage of wire and plywood.

I won't send my next color film to Eastman at Australia. The mail clerk found the airmail rate would be $2.80 each way!

Thurs., 10.18.1945, Saipan

Dave, Walt O'Connell and I have been working up at the darkroom almost every evening. Last night we developed four rolls and made over a hundred prints. We really don't make any money on it because what we charge the fellows just covers the cost of paper and chemicals. The main advantage to us is that whenever we print somebody's pictures we always make prints for ourselves. That way we get a chance to see all the pictures men in our outfit have taken and we also make our own copies if we want. In some respects the results area a little crude, but they're passable and pretty good for the amount of equipment we have. If I do decide to hang on to and use my black and white film, I'll still send that to you. A 35-mm. film is a little too long to develop by hand and we don't have a tank. Then too, we can't produce fine a grain size as we'd want for films to be enlarged.

Clyde Helzer left yesterday. He and four others go to a processing area and then they'll start home in a week or so. All of them had at least 70 points.

I have to escort one of our Gooks up to the native hospital as I understand it his wife is having a baby.

A fellow just came in to change a tire and I asked him if his ring wasn't a City College [Baltimore, MD high school] ring. It was- his home is on Belair Road. We chatted awhile-don't seem to know the same people, but we do know the same places. Such is life.

Sat., 10.20.1945, Saipan
We printed up a set of 14 pictures showing the highway billboards and some scenes of the island. Now almost everyone wants copies so we have had orders for 70 sets of 14 each or a total of 980 prints! That'll mean a lot of work, but it will also mean a clear profit of $9.00 for each of us and besides that orders are still coming in faster than we can fill them. Last night we worked from 6:00 PM 'til 10:00 and made 244 prints. (That's the most we've done in one night so far.) Even at that rate our labor is only earning us 61 cents an hour-we should be worth more than that. I guess we'll have to improve our mass-production methods. We can't even put more time in on Sunday or other times during the day because the room lets too much light in and besides it's too hot to work in there during the day. In fact it's hot enough at night. We usually take a can of cold fruit juice or some Cokes or beer for our rest periods. The main bottleneck now in our mass-production is cutting paper. The paper is in large sheets and we have to use a razor blade to cut it to 3 ½ x 2 ½. So this afternoon Dave and I are going to ride over to the Air Corps and try to "scrounge up" a paper cutter. The Air Corps is leaving here and they have a lot of stuff to get rid of.

Sat., 10.20.1945, Saipan
We are still taking pictures of the clever billboards.

Bush is our "chemist" in the darkroom, I'm the chief paper cutter, and Walt exposes the negatives. Yours truly is also the efficiency expert and always full of new ideas!

Sun., 10.22.1945, Saipan
I went up to the dark room, built some shelves and finished a stool Dave made. By then the prints that we made last night were dry and I put them under a press to dry. Walt runs a generator that gives our area electricity- he starts 4:00 to midnight shift this week, so he won't be there.

I had a lot of mail today! Letter from home and a large envelope with my law notes. (If I can only find time now.)

Tues., 10.23.1945, Saipan
Since you're speaking of spare time let's take up the subject of "law study" first. You're quite right in saying I should use my spare moments to study, and my intentions are good. (I wrote home for my law notes when I first arrived and they came last week.) However, here at work the Gooks have to pound on steel wheels with large hammers and that combined with the jabbering and the fact that I have to sign a voucher about every three minutes (when drivers come and leave) plus answering all the fool questions everyone can ask- it not only doesn't leave much time to study, but what time there is isn't very good for concentration. But I do have the notes and intend to use them whenever I get the chance. It's too bad I didn't have them for the ride over but I'll have them for the ride back. Now for my dating native girls. I get a kick out of it every time I think of it. I told Dave that you had asked me not to date any native girls and he almost split his sides laughing. I wouldn't want to if I could. I didn't and don't want to date other pretty, clean, nice American girls other than you. But the funny part is there isn't a choice for anyone to get even near any natives. Most of the native women and girls work in the laundry, hospital, gov't offices, etc. but they can't leave there during the day and all hours except those whose work is spent in the native village compound. The compound is all enclosed with barb-wire, guarded by native police and U.S. M.P's. No natives are out of the compound at night for

any reason. The fences are just littered with signs of "Keep Out", "Off Limits", and "Keep Moving". Why even the native farmers and their families who have the little shacks are collected by trucks every evening and have to live within the compound at night and do their farming by day. Since I left Seattle I've spoken to only one female and that was a Jap. girl. She was a nurse in the native (military gov't) hospital and since she spoke both Japanese and Korean I explained (by use of a Jap. phrase book) for her to tell one of my boys to bring his card with him every day he was to have his eye treated. Now does that solve the date problem? When I told Dave about this date business he said his girl did this too. Dave had written that he and I had made pretty nice foot-lockers to keep our clothes in and his girl replied "That's nice. Maybe you'll bring it home with you." Now, "nice" to us means as compared to bring something out of a duffle-bag. Besides, how would he carry it home? Then too, we want to come home and live out of closets and chests of drawers, not foot-lockers!

I got a long letter from Hank. Believe it or not, the guy is going to stay in the Navy. He says liquor and women are plentiful and that's what he likes so he's staying in. Now he's down at San Juan, Porto [sic] Rico and seems to like the life there. Lou, it seems, is not in this part of the world, but nobody seems to know just where.

Mrs. Nauss' little boy doesn't have a lot of suntan, nor Atabrine yellow but I have something else. The fingernails of my right hand are becoming very dark-stained from all the darkroom work and having my right hand in developer so much.

Man alive but I have a stack of letters here. My writing case was getting so full that I decided to bring your letters to work with me and answer all of the things I intended to answer for a long time. Then I can again close my writing case. Yes, I still discard old letters-even yours.

So, you got a raise did you? Well aren't you the one! You won't let me get one unless you get one too! You vixen!

Maybe I'm not up on my rings. The plain gold band sounds OK to me, but I've always thought a guard was just another ring. In that case there would be your engagement ring, wedding ring and guard ring. That would make three rings on one finger and would be a bit crowded and cluttered up wouldn't it, or am I mistaken as usual? After we're married (sounds nice doesn't it?) you probably won't wear the Theta Chi pin very often (not many seem to.) I wonder if it couldn't be made into a fairly nice looking (and different) dinner ring by having the pin taken off the back and a plain gold band attached. I've never seen or heard of it being done before, but the size and shape should be OK and it isn't every wife who can wear her hubby's old frat pin as a smart, different dinner ring. It might be worth a try.

Now, as we were speaking of the great Henderson (as Johnny Archer calls Bud) so Bud passed you up on the street with just a nod. Don't feel badly-that's Bud. You have to really get to know him to realize that. He has passed me like that too. He starts thinking like that and doesn't seem to realize where he is, who he speaks to, etc. I can't understand it because he never seems to think deeply enough on any subject to become that absorbed, but that's how it is.

Saipan is the assembly point for troops going back to the States. We now have 17,000 waiting to go home.

Fri., 10.26.1945, Saipan
There just isn't time for anything anymore. Things seem rushed at work and even my spare hours are rushed. At least now I think I've talked the outfit into giving me a 4th man for the tire shop. I mean another man would make four including myself. I'm here during the day and one fellow takes over from 2:00 'til 11:00 PM and a third from 11:00 PM to 7:00 AM. The two night men are just more or less night watchmen and do sign driver's dispatches. But 90% of the work is during the day- so I think I'm getting another man to help out. Then

he can get the Gooks early in the morning and I can sleep later and work from 8:00 AM 'til 4:00 PM. Men who work in the supply room are always bothered by requests for clothes, men asking about laundry, etc. It's the same with the mail clerk. Everybody always wants to know if he has any mail and if not, why not. Now we at "NOB, Inc. (Nauss, O'Connell, Bush) are bothered day and night by people who want to know when their films and prints will be ready. We only accept work from the 470th and still we have much more than we can handle and we can't get help because the size of the darkroom and amount of equipment won't stand more than three men at a time. Dave and Walt just split our roll and our first split just amounted to $14.00 each.

Mon.10.29.1945, Saipan
We drove 40 miles sightseeing, took plenty of photographs and even found an old Jap command post. Later we went swimming, as usual.

Tues., 10.30.1945, Saipan
Thank you for the information you sent about a possible patent office position. See if you can find out what type of exam would be needed and if any old exams area available to study as well as when the exam is given.

Dwight Gault is a contact. It would be in Washington. I already have a civil service rating (since I'm still technically on furlough from Ordnance) and besides that veterans get a ____________.

Thurs., 11.1.1945, Saipan
We printed out negatives of 19 shots of the island before the war. Now we will sell 100 sets at $2.00 per. We are also working on a plan to make Christmas cards. We've had some problems with our processing. We had whole bottles of our developer go bad in the bottles due to the heat and the brackish water causes some of our prints to go haywire and fresh drinking water is too scarce to use as we need gallons to wash the prints. We get our photographic paper for free since we have officers who know they'll get prints if they give us

the paper. Our best source is a Lt. assigned to help the Air Corps leave and he knows where and who to ask when things like that are being left behind instead of carried back to the States. He can get "bribes" from officers who can't locate paper. We have a self-imposed rule to only do work for the 470th and even that is too much. Anyone else has to produce paper, chemicals, etc. or barter as in one case we traded prints for a fifth of rye. It's a good brand of stateside stuff too! We've gotten a landslide of darkroom supplies- had trouble fitting it all into the darkroom. Fans, trays, chemicals, automatic timing clock, printers, and 25 gross of 20"x 20" paper- over $500 worth of paper alone! The other night one roll of film was ruined and we thought it had been our fault. But when we told the fellow he just laughed and said he didn't expect it to be any good. He had bought that roll of film two years ago in Alaska! Is it any wonder my hair is thin! Oh, at lunch some fellow from another outfit tried to sell us some photographic paper. The highwayman wanted $10.00 for one gross of 10"x10". We just said no and didn't tell him that so far all our paper hasn't cost us a thing. We just have some officers who know we'll give them prints if they get us paper.

Speaking of Christmas- this noon my first package arrived. The family sent a package of three cans from - Hutzler's fudge, fruitcake and salted nuts.

Would I mind living in Washington? Heck no! I've always said I'd like to live there and besides it is close enough to Baltimore to run back and forth now and then. I'm all for that dear. Besides, after the war workers leave there should be plenty of apts., etc.

I'm watching the Gooks playing a checkers-type game. Dave says it looks like a Turkish game he'd heard about with a name like "Hoonay". They move stones around, many can play and each man uses six stones. The board looks something like three squares within each other and diagonal lines extending to the corners.

Sat., 11.3.1945, Saipan
We're now spending seven nights a week in our darkroom.

Tues., 11.6.1945, Saipan
The profits from our darkroom aren't mounting as fast as we had hoped.

My family did not react too favorably to our Mexican trip idea. They pointed out that the wedding and furniture will both cost money and two weeks wouldn't be long enough for the trip to Mexico.

If I go into Civil Service I would get 30 days a year in leave time.

A few of my friends have already been thru Meade and didn't get their furloughs and the separation business only took them about 48 hours.

Fri., 11.9.1945, Saipan
It seems Geo. Jr. came thru the typhoon OK with the exception of having his belongings scattered and soaked.

I can't get any peace! I just had to stop to accept a roll of film for printing and developing-that'll be 65 cents- 25 cents for developing and five cents for each of the eight prints. Bush and I have bunks next to each other and that forms the office of "NOB, Inc.". One hour from now is the deadline on our new ordering system. So many fellows want photos showing scenes of the island that we made a set of ten from Bush's negatives. Then we posted the set of ten pictures on the bulletin board with a company roster and a notice for those wanting the set to just mark after their names the number of sets desired at 50 cents per. Already over 50 sets are ordered- and we're still limiting it to the 470th. That way we can set up and do some mass production instead of doing the same set over and over.

Please don't worry about getting anything for the darkroom. There's really nothing we could use except more time to do the work. Then too, we sort of pride ourselves that the company operates with no overhead whatsoever.

I'm at the moment on another of my "no smoking" sprees. Three days ago I decided to quit for about a week just to reassure myself that I'm not bound by the habit. I haven't smoked a pipe or cigarettes for three days and I can't say that I feel any better or worse for it. The only thing I notice is that without a pipe, tobacco, and lighter I have more room in my pockets for other junk. I got a new pipe a few weeks ago. It's one of those Kirsten-metal jobs. I've never cared for the looks of them, but so many people claim they are so good. The P.X. here got some and since they were about half the price they are in the States, I decided to try one. Pretty good, but no better than my others.

I was surprised to see the forms and all the dope on the Patent Office business. I don't think it would do a bit of harm to get the application in as soon as possible and I'll send it on to you as soon as I can figure out all the answers and get hold of a typewriter. There's one thing that has me up a tree 'tho. It should be notarized and on the list of people not authorized to give the oath are Army officers and post office employees and I doubt if there are any civilian notaries on this rock. The main thing that worries me is the part about "engineering graduates". After all, two years of engineering is a long way from an engineering graduate! And they don't seem to care about law education. We'll try it, but don't get your hopes up too high.

As for the Richmond or Washington deal either would be OK with me. As for knowing anyone in Richmond, all I know is Connie (my cuz. and her husband).

Mon., 11.12.1945, Saipan
I just finished a big discussion that is if you can call making an explanation to a bunch of jabbering Koreans a discussion! No, it wasn't about the soap ration this time. The current discussion was about lunch. They used to eat between 11:00 and 12:00 and now working hours for some shifts have been

changed and our Gooks have to eat at 12:00 and be back to work at 1:00 and they don't like it one bit! They rant and rave that they get hungry before 12:00, but all I can tell them is that it's "T.S." because so do I. The colored mess Sgt. of their mess hall just came down and said one of our Gooks tried to force his way in early and they had to wave a carbine at him to make him stop. So I had to go to great lengths of basic English to explain that they can't eat until the mess Sgt. tells them he's ready. This is just like running a sort of kindergarten except that they are strong and work hard. I've given up attempting to teach them English except for helping them with a word now and then. There are just too many things to be done without wasting time on them.

Another packet of newspaper pages came yesterday Thanks a million sweetheart. I feel I'm keeping well-posted on the affairs of Baltimore as well as Saipan.

The photo business is coming along 'tho the set to be printed from paper negatives (that we expected to make a lot of money from) fell thru when we found we couldn't get clear prints out of them. To date NOB has been operating about a month and we've cleared $25.00 (That isn't too bad considering I have worked for less than $25.00 per month at a full-time job). We have about $10.00 on hand in change and about $20.00 worth of prints made on order but not yet called for.

Equipment and materials just seem to fall like "manna from Heaven". Before we finished making a paper-cutter we heard about an abandoned one and made a wild dash in a jeep at night clear to the other end of the island and finally located it. It isn't bad either- the corners it cuts aren't quite square, but I think we can fix that.

We've seen several places where we'd like to try to make a panorama, several shots pushed together to make a wide view. But we needed a tripod. Last night we were talking about making a tripod and one fellow said "Wait!" and dashed out. A few minutes later he was back with a nice wooden tripod like engineers use for a survey level, etc. All we had to do was take it apart, cut the screws off, and weld on a screw that would fit the cameras. It's too bad we can't take some of this junk back to the States with us. We'll hate to leave all the possessions that range from Jeeps and motor scooters and sailboats to monkeys but "You can't take it with you." And I guess we'll be glad enough just to get ourselves home.

The current packet of *The Sun* also arrived just as fast as airmail in spite of a three-cent stamp. A lot of fellows noticed it and nobody can understand it. It doesn't seem to work that way with the color film. The first one hasn't arrived yet and it's had 45 days. The only thing I can think of is that maybe Eastman didn't return it by airmail. The rats! What do they think I enclosed 18 cents worth of stamps for? Nuts!

Today a lot of outfits are taking the day off as the holiday that should have been yesterday. But the docks are still loading and unloading ships so our trucks must work and if the trucks work the tire shop must work.

Here's something you might do. We have a whole can of film-45 feet of it and a foot wide! And it's color film. We even have the various things to develop the stuff, but we don't know how. How about asking Eastman or Stark if they have any printed dope on how to develop and print Kodacolor film? Not Kodachrome, but Kodacolor. It doesn't give as true color as Kodachrome, but with all that free film we'd like to try it out.

P.S. NOB, Inc. just declared another split of $10.00 each. I just love to hear that silver roll in!

Thurs., 11.15.1945, Saipan
Please don't compare and check the workmanship of our prints too closely. We're operating a darkroom under conditions where most sane people wouldn't even attempt it. Eastman, Stark, etc. in their neat air-conditioned places would be appalled. We could almost write a book on our darkroom troubles in the tropics! Chemicals for developing and printing

should be 68° F and even with a fan we've never been able to get our darkroom below 85°F! Even the water is warm since the storage tank is in the sun all day. Besides, instead of mixing solutions and washing prints in nice clear water we have to use brackish water that is unfit to drink and little better than sea water. We spray the place every night for the better health of all the ants, spiders, lizards, grasshoppers, etc. In spite of all that we often have to fish grasshoppers and other bugs out of our developing trays! After developing a roll we hang the strip of film up to dry overnight. We couldn't understand the tiny marks on the film until we saw a lizard walk down a strip from the rafter! As far as the space! The darkroom is 6 ft. x 6 ft.. x 10 ft. high and includes a sink (made from a tin gas drum cut in half), two tables, two stools and three men. Just a bit crowded. Then there's the current. Here the current for about every ¼ mi. square is furnished by an oil-burning generator and lights flicker, fade, go off, blow fuses, etc. When the lights are off we can at least develop films, but reading films and all the other things must be done by candlelight. And with the lights out we just can't print any pictures and have to suspend operations. "These are times that try men's souls." Dave says some of his prints are getting a bit brown already.

My temporary writing case is a copy of *Coronet* I carry in my pocket to keep photos, incoming and outgoing mail, etc. from getting too dog-eared. Every now and then I get time to read an article. I haven't done so well and I'm still lugging around the September issue.

This morning we had a regular Korean-Anglo peace confab here. I wish I could get a motion picture with sound of a session like that! What a scream! Our "number one boy" asked me to come outside with him and there I found all of our Gooks squatting around in a circle. Standing in the center was an envoy they dug up somewhere who spoke very bad but almost understandable English. He bowed, greeted me in all sorts of ways, wanted to know how long I had been on Saipan, how soon I hoped to go home, etc. Meanwhile he and I stood in the center with all the Gooks squatting around and taking in every word as if they understood it or not. Then he proceeded to try to snow me under with a long song and dance about how the Koreans never loved the Japs, how the Japs brought them here, how the Japs made Koreans, Japs, and Chamorras [Spanish-speaking natives] all work together whereas Americans let Koreans work in groups, Japs in groups, etc., how hard they had to work for the Japs, and how easy we work them and how much better we treat them than the Japs did. He spread it on thick and while I took it all in and thought things like "If you hadn't helped the Japs we wouldn't have had this mess to begin with." and the reports that when given authority the Koreans had often been more brutal to Americans than the Japs. Well, it all ended up that they wanted me to speak to the Capt. about letting them put up a tent beside the tire shop, draw rations and cook their own lunch every day instead of going up to the mess hall tent that is run for them. They figure that way they'll be able to save some extra canned goods and take the loot back to the native compound. It's out of the question-there's no doubt about that. They could put a tent up and we have a tank of drinking water, but the Army won't let them build an extra mess hall when one isn't needed. A sump or grease trap would have to be built for wastewater, a ration and bread truck would have to bring food every day, a garbage truck would have to stop here, and they would need stoves, pots, pans, etc. Now when they eat oranges, etc. they throw stuff around and I have to make them clean up. With a whole mess hall next door they'd have this place like a dump in nothing flat!

It's always something! The Gooks just came back from lunch and with them came an MP jeep. It seems one of the Gooks under our care who works in another part of the motor pool was a bit drunk (Lord knows where he got the stuff, probably *sake* made from rice). At any rate he got into trouble with a G.I. and the G.I. knocked a few of his teeth out. Now all sorts of reports will go back and forth between here, the M.P.s and the Military Gov't. I guess he'll get fired and end up digging ditches. Such names- this joker is Hohng Janng Hwann.

It seems the only difference is the speed difference between train and air from the East Coast to the West Coast. Maybe if that's the case it would be a good idea to save the pennies and put them in the baby's piggy bank. As I said before it isn't the speed that counts so much as it is the regularity. Do as you think best darling. I'll try a few letters Free and see how they get there. That way I'd be able to save twice as much as you on postage-but you do write more often than I- God Bless You.

Speaking of coin of the realm-NOB split $4.00 each least night. (We don't like to leave much cash around to tempt anyone.) That makes $39.00 per. The other day I sent home a money order of $100.00 for deposit-that's in addition to the $25.00 I'm having sent home every month. It may be a long road but we'll get there honey.

Last night we printed some pictures and there were several with two fellows in our outfit and two native girls. We were amazed and wondered where they were able to get near enough to native girls to pose with them. Then we saw "Cliff Club" in one picture and we realized that there are two native girls as waitresses in this Red Cross canteen.

What kind of stripes do I wear? Well, I don't wear any. It's this way: stripes don't matter a bit around here. They only thing they are good for is the pay. Very few below Sgt. ever put stripes on fatigues and over here almost nobody wears them on fatigues and what's the use of putting them on suntans when I've only worn suntans once since we left Seattle and then it was because I washed all my fatigues at once and didn't have anything else to wear. But what I should wear is this: [two strips with a capital T underneath]

My afternoon assistant just came down. He takes the Gooks home and works from 3:00 PM 'til 11:00 PM.

The news (rumor) is that names of men with two years' service went in today. Now, don't get excited. Get down off that chair and stop yelling. I said it's only a rumor.

Sat., 11.17.1945, Saipan
You must have heard by now of the point score being dropped to 55 points or four years' service. I wonder how long it'll take to get those men out and start on the three-year men. See today's date? The 17th. It was three years ago today that I went into the Army. I was sworn in on the 17th and left for Meade the 24th.

Oh, big news! The first set of slides arrived. And they are swell! Only one is a little dark and that isn't bad since I got 19 on the roll instead of 18. With all these pictures you'll know every inch of Saipan as well as I do before long. I'll send along the usual list to describe the slides and then I'll put one or two in each airmail letter. I'll put prints in a few Free letters, but I won't trust the slides to Free mail. You know what took so long with the slides? The jerk at Eastman returned them by first class mail and returned my stamps!

Speaking of postage- no I won't write any V-mail and neither will you. We had a notice about two weeks ago that V-mail is over, washed up, finished, and not accepted any more.

Yes, I heard about the G.I. bill being raised, but unless I'm mistaken it is now $75 single and $90 married.

As for pictures of me, I'll enclose a trial shot Dave took of me to try out our new tripod, indoor lighting and time exposure.

We did have to do some wiring to put the fan in the darkroom, but it was well worth it. It's a combination electric heater and fan with a switch to make it blow out hot air, but I doubt if we'll ever need to turn the heat on around here!

Not everybody gets me out of bed to ask about pictures. Walt and Dave get their share too. Ours is a partnership with Walt as vice-president in charge of printing, Dave is vice-president in charge of chemicals and I am vice-president in charge of paper. It's my department at fault when you see cockeyed paper or paper with a torn edge (the latter we call "prints with a fringe on top"). The Christmas card idea is just starting to get under way and already we have a new brainstorm. We made our own negative for the cards by scratching lettering and design on a piece of black film so the light comes thru and prints the letters Now we'd like to do the same for a large map of the island and draw lines between the map location and a print of that area. It would be a lot of work and each copy would have to be about 20 in. x 24 in. The Christmas cards don't say "Merry Christmas" but "Season's Greetings" so we can get the Jewish trade too. If we can ever find time the three of us would also like to make more personal cards for ourselves.

Lord, I hope I'm not getting henpecked already, but I'll agree not to let the boys take me on a boat the night before our wedding. I'm no little tin god, but I'm not quite the cad and bounder that your paragraph makes me appear. OK, you win. I'll be all yours, but you better look out! I'm coming home after no loving for a long, long time and you'll have to make up for lots of lost time. You better get lots of sleep and rest when you hear I'm on my way home!

All the rest of my life every time I see or hear of mold I'll think of the tropics. Maybe I'll even be moldy when I get home. All leather, even billfolds, etc. get moldy. I had to get some pipe tobacco the other day and I had to buy <u>six</u> packages before I got <u>one</u> that wasn't moldy. (The P.X. takes it back.) And all the packages were wrapped in cellophane too!

I don't know how I'll like the shoulder length hair, but you know 'lil Allen- I'll tell you if I don't like it. Remember the bangs and the card from Yale? Or could you ever forget?

Mon., 11.19.1945, Saipan
The watch is one that one of the Gooks wanted to buy today. He was willing to pay $80.00 for it and even had the money counted out and shoving it in my hand. I don't know where he got the

$80.00 but he seems to deal in watches and ______- all he can get his hands on. The P.X. gets $28.00 Swiss jobs about one or two per month and several times he (knowing they cost the G.I. $28.00) paid $35.00 for them. I guess he sells them to other Gooks for about $50.00 I tried to explain that I'll sell mine for $100.00 or $72.00 and a new P.X. watch. Bush and the other fellow think I've gone "island happy" for not taking $80.00 but I like my watch and I'm in no hurry to get rid of it 'tho I do hate to pass up a good deal.

Tues., 11.20.1945, Saipan
The biggest bit of news is that I weakened and sold my watch today. You'd think I needed money or something, but here's how I figured. As I told you before, it started acting queerly there for awhile. This place and type of life isn't healthy for a good watch. The gold was worn on the edges, etc. of my watch, and the band (flexible gold link) was stretching out of shape and would have to be replaced soon. So I figured that if I could buy it for $65.00, wear it for three years, and then sell it for $95.00 it wasn't so bad.

Yes, I sold it for $30.00 more than I paid for it three years ago. Now I'll buy one for $20 or $25 from one of the fellows and send the balance home for deposit. I'm already wearing another watch on a free trial. Dave calls me a "filthy capitalist".

Thurs., 11.22.1945, Saipan [Thanksgiving]
"Tomorrow no chop chop." "All the same same like Sunday." That's what I told my boys-that we wouldn't work today.

If you thought you were getting few pictures of me, well you'll get even fewer now. You see, our barber left on points and I finally agreed to let Dave cut my hair if he'd agree to let me cut his! Now neither of us is fit for photographs! He gave me even a shorter cut than my first G.I. at Fort Meade and I told him to only trim it! I only trimmed his, but there are lots of uneven spots.

Eight of our boys have plenty to be thankful for today. They were told last night to turn their stuff in today and they're going right to the ship instead of spending several weeks at the replacement depot. There are eleven aircraft carriers and a hospital ship out in Tanapag Harbor now and they should get most of the 55 pointers and four-year men done by Christmas. The glad word is that they're counting length of service up to Dec. 1st so that'll put me in the 3-year class whereas the Sept. 10th deal would have given me two years.

Well, this is my fourth Thanksgiving dinner in the Army. We had turkey, cranberry sauce, mashed potatoes, peas, corn, dressing, ice-cream cake, pumpkin pie, etc. and a carton of cigs per. Not bad, but who wouldn't rather be home- with you.

Fri., 11.23.1945, Saipan
I hope the results of men getting home are as good as the reports! All the four-year men in our outfit are leaving Sun. on a ship that
got here in only 11 days! That means they'll get home in plenty of time for Christmas.

That's more like it! Two letters from my betrothed and also two envelopes full of hometown papers! Love is a wonderful thing, even if your love is 8,000 miles away. Did you read in the papers about the plane that got there on a nonstop flight from Guam in 35 hours? That really only makes me 35 hours away from you since Guam is only 70 miles from us.

As usual, you're right about my not sending so many prints by air and sending some regular mail- but as is often the case, I'm ahead of you and I've already started that. What a pair we are!

Sun., 11.25.1945, Saipan
Glad you were getting out with the crowd a bit even if you didn't have your own man. I don't doubt that you were "flying low" but why on earth mixing wine with highballs? It's no wonder you couldn't take that; few people could. We still have our unopened bottle of rye- I think we'll save that for Christmas. Our beer ration has been about doubled so we drink about two bottles every night.

Now on every Saturday night we get a quart of Australian beer each and such stuff. It's good- in fact it's great, but it's about 12% and a quart at a time is enough to put you on your ear. Last night the quart of beer combined with the heat of the darkroom had us feeling no pain.

NOB is coming along quite well now and every time we seem to get caught up on work a new landslide hits us. That guy Nauss finally got on the ball and scaled a big map of the island down to a six-inch size, drew it on thin paper, and then went over it with India ink. Now we hope to be able to reproduce it and then you'll be able to understand more about the strange places like Camp Susupe and Marpi Point.

Mon., 11.26.1945, Saipan
Most of the Christmas cards that were ordered are finished now so last night we tried to make some more personal ones for ourselves. Those we produced in bulk had a scene of the island in the center and we decided to use those ourselves too since it seems to look best. We did print (at a special rate) a personal photo in place of the island scene, but I don't like it as well that way. Oh yes, the photo business is going cutthroat. One fellow started his own darkroom in the outfit next-door to us. However, he works alone and can't turn out the volume of work that we can. He has been accepting trade from men in our outfit, but I think NOB can keep things under control because he is low on paper and is dickering to buy paper from us. Then about a week ago he acquired a small developing set and got us to show them how it's done-give them a little paper, etc. because they wanted to "learn just for our own films so we can take it up as a hobby when we get home." It seems now that one of their henchmen got an outside order of six films to be developed and printed. They gave us the rolls for development alone and then gave the negatives to the "upstart" for prints. When we found out about that deal we blew our stacks-because it's harder and longer to develop a roll than to print the pictures and developing only brings 25 cents whereas printing the same roll takes about half the time and brings 40 cents. I guess they thought we were foolish when we sold them a whole gross box of paper for $3.00.

Allen H. Nauss, aviation cadet

Military police, Fort Meyer, VA

Truck gunner, Brownwood, TX

Traveling to unknown destination

Bags ready to move from Camp Lewis to Fort Lawton, Washington

SGT. Tester and gear, *U.S.S. George S. Julian*

U.S.S. George G. Julian troop ship, heading to Saipan

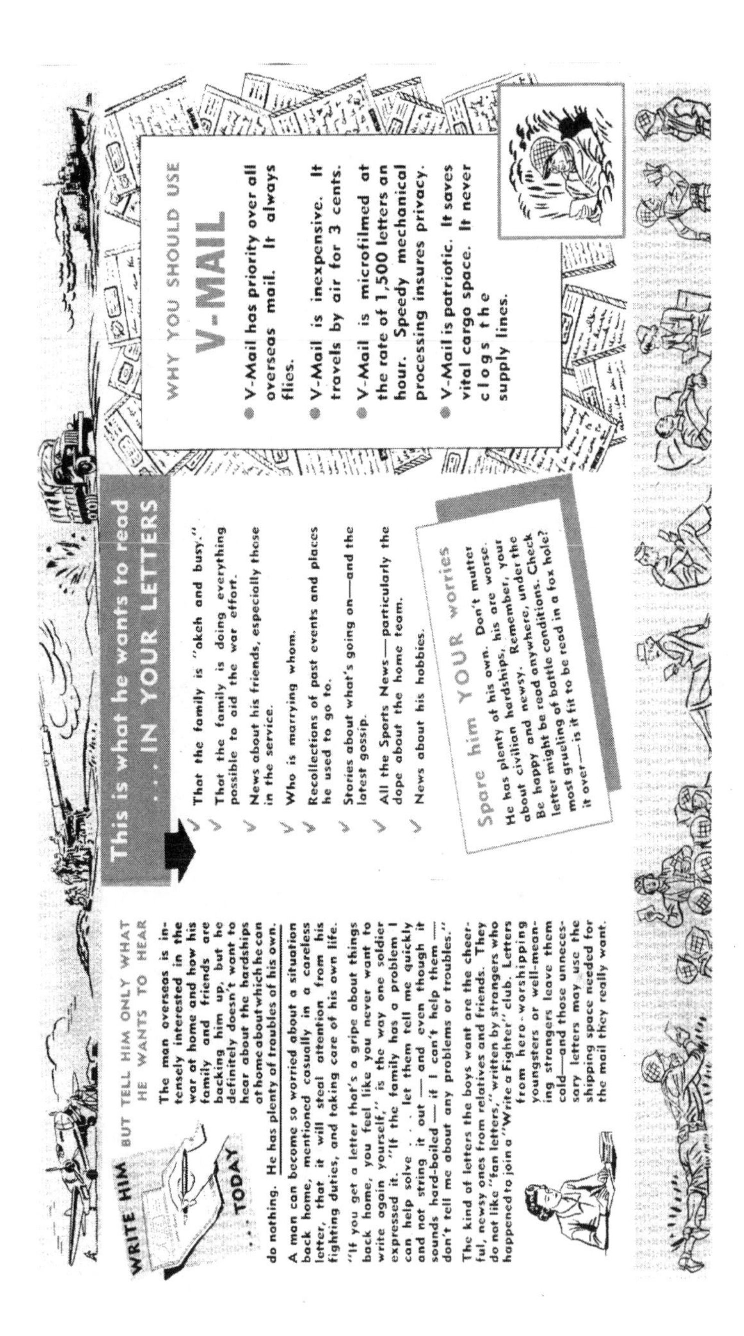

WRITE HIM ... TODAY

BUT TELL HIM ONLY WHAT HE WANTS TO HEAR

The man overseas is intensely interested in the war at home and how his family and friends are backing him up, but he definitely doesn't want to hear about the hardships at home about which he can do nothing. He has plenty of troubles of his own.

A man can become so worried about a situation back home, mentioned casually in a careless letter, that it will steal attention from his fighting duties, and taking care of his own life.

"If you get a letter that's a gripe about things back home, you feel like you never want to write again yourself," is the way one soldier expressed it. "If the family has a problem I can help solve . . . let them tell me quickly and not string it out — and even though it sounds hard-boiled — if I can't help them — don't tell me about any problems or troubles."

The kind of letters the boys want are the cheerful, newsy ones from relatives and friends. They do not like "fan letters," written by strangers who happened to join a "Write a Fighter" club. Letters from hero-worshipping youngsters or well-meaning strangers leave them cold—and those unnecessary letters may use the shipping space needed for the mail they really want.

This is what he wants to read . . . IN YOUR LETTERS

- That the family is "okeh and busy."
- That the family is doing everything possible to aid the war effort.
- News about his friends, especially those in the service.
- Who is marrying whom.
- Recollections of past events and places he used to go to.
- Stories about what's going on—and the latest gossip.
- All the Sports News—particularly the dope about the home team.
- News about his hobbies.

Spare him YOUR worries

He has plenty of his own. Don't mutter about civilian hardships, his are worse. Be happy and newsy. Remember, your letter might be read anywhere, under the most grueling of battle conditions. Check it over—is it fit to be read in a fox hole?

WHY YOU SHOULD USE

V-MAIL

- V-Mail has priority over all overseas mail. It always flies.
- V-Mail is inexpensive. It travels by air for 3 cents.
- V-Mail is microfilmed at the rate of 1,500 letters an hour. Speedy mechanical processing insures privacy.
- V-Mail is patriotic. It saves vital cargo space. It never clogs the supply lines.

V-Mail instructions

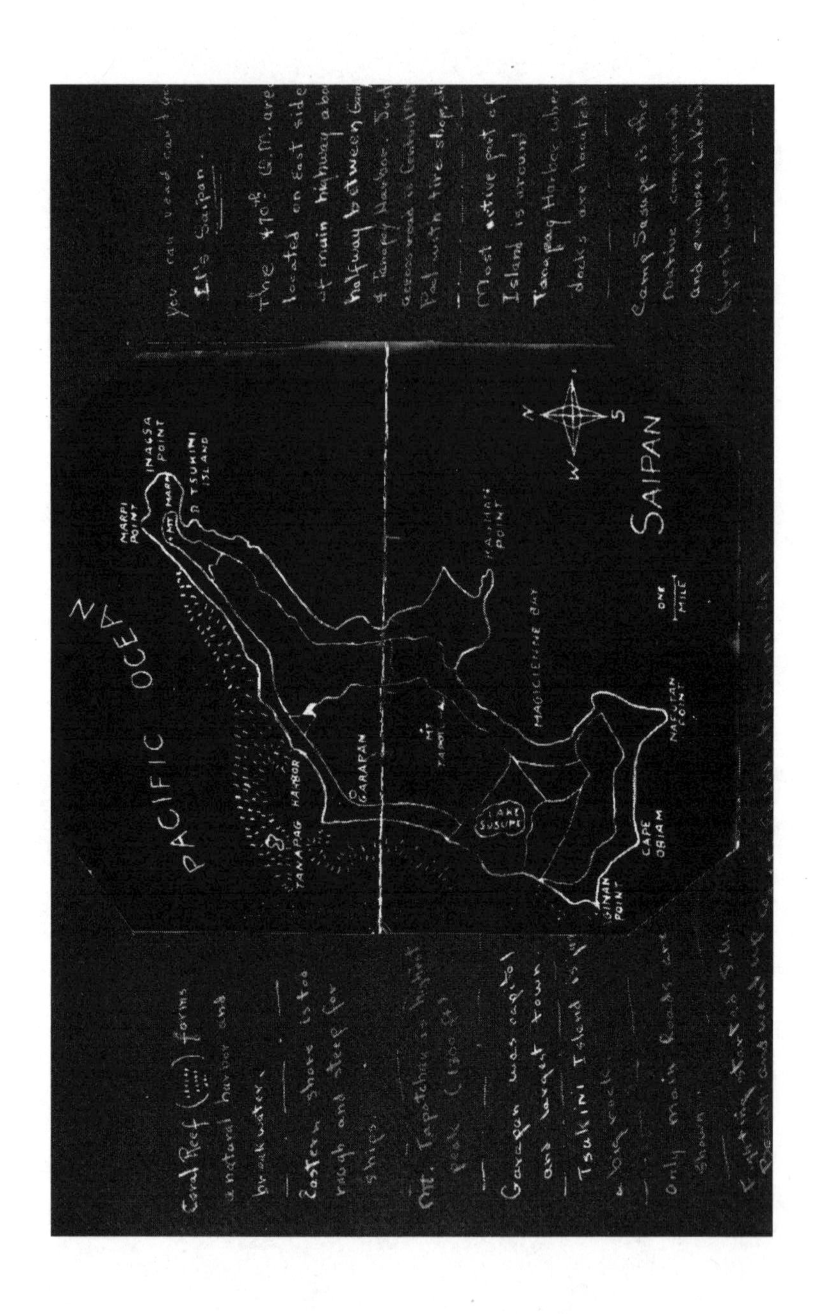

Allen's hand-drawn map of Saipan

Nauss & Korean conscript truck tire repair crew, Saipan

Base housing and Sanders, Saipan

Pre-war native hut, Saipan

"Cliff Club" Red Cross canteen, Saipan

Native girls and Red Cross worker, Saipan

Japanese prisoners of war, building a day building, Saipan

Dave Bush

Walt O'Connell

B-29 bombers, Saipan

Military billboards, Saipan

Atabrine sign, Saipan

Red Cross "Cliff Club", Saipan

"Repple Depple" soldiers from Replacement Depot traveling by truck to return home by ship, Saipan

Japanese prisoners of war, building a dayroom, Saipan

Hospital ship (white ship) and others, Tanapag Harbor, Saipan

"NOB" Christmas card

Fourth Marine cemetery, Saipan

What they didn't realize is that we have chemicals that they depend on. So we now have two other outfits in business against NOB-but we've built up a trade. We still have more business than we can handle, are well-stocked for paper and chemicals, have never paid any overhead, and we can put either or both of the others out of business in about a week by just not selling them the stuff they need. NOB rules the photograph's roost on Saipan.
If Odie is having trouble getting prints made you can tell him to send them to me if you want (no charge for friends). He could send films or negatives or both and I could mail them back one day after I get them. Direct mail should be marked "Inter-Island". If you have any negatives you want printed, old or new, just drop them in with a letter and "NOB" is glad to be of service.

NOB isn't the only business with too much trade- the tire shop too. We're only supposed to furnish good tires in trade for flats to trucks from our motor pool. However, I've helped out some other outfits and given them tires, but now the word has got around that we are the only motor pool on the island where the labor is done by Gooks. Now people are bringing tires all the way from the other end of the island to trade them with us instead of fixing them themselves as they are supposed to. As a result, our work has almost doubled in the past two weeks and ______ and air compressors are breaking down. So now I have to turn people away and tell them to go fix their own tires or get their own crew of Gooks. I think when I get home we'll have to get roller skates-I'm getting tired of seeing tires.

What are you gals doing? Trying to steal our stuff on that silver dollar business? It doesn't seem to make as much sense as our bet tho'. When we made the bet none of us was very eager to get married, so we figured the first would have to pay for his folly (in silver dollars).

I thought I had answered about money or humidor. I think we'll have much more use for the money than the humidor don't you honey? I've done very well without a humidor for the past 26 years, but I have needed money now and then, so I think it's the best choice.

Well, it's 3:45 PM and my assistant has taken the Gooks home. Now it's about time for me to "forward plod my weary nag" then shower, eat dinner, and see how much work NOB is expected to turn out tonight. See you later Vixen old girl.

6:00 PM Hello again. What do you know- I just got my second package to arrive on the sun-baked isle of Saipan! And it's from my chick!! Now I'm just like a little boy-open it now or wait 'til Christmas? I sort of think I'll wait because Christmas away from you and home is bad enough, but if there isn't anything left to open it would be just another day. Thanks a million dearest. You are sweet enough to be...my wife.

Tues., 11.27.1945, Saipan
Had a letter from home today and it says Geo. Jr has left Okinawa and gone to Shikudo, unable to verify correct name[sic-Shokudo]-near the main island.

What do you mean about you at a summer camp this summer? I'll be home by summer if I have to walk- and it'll be a long, wet walk too. Last week the *Stars and Stripes* said they expect to start sending two-year men home by March so that means all the three-year men will be home by then. I'll be home before summer-don't worry about that!

Sun., 12.2.1945, Saipan
We've been trying for weeks to get a radio for our darkroom to entertain us while we work. Well, still no radio, but the other day we did get a nice new phonograph with a stack of platters. So, for the past few nights we've had music while we work 'tho it is some trouble to wind it, select records and change needles in the dark. Last night as we walked into the darkroom, Walt said "Look!" A can of developer was on a ledge along the wall and curled around the can was the largest tarantula I've ever seen! We all backed out of there fast and wondered what to do. Our only weapon was a broom and there wasn't much room to swing that. We had to kill it because we didn't want to be shut

up in a darkroom when we knew there was a tarantula in there. A rattlesnake is bad enough, but at least they make a noise. To make a long story short, Dave and Walt wouldn't even go inside and I was elected to do battle with the broom. I missed the critter about four times and he disappeared. Then we were in a jam! We didn't want to start work until we were sure he was dead so we sprayed the place all over with aerosol, but that didn't bring him out of hiding. Then Dave said it might sound goofy but spiders are supposed to like music so we started the phonograph. Well, we, or rather, I, did (they wouldn't come inside) but I should talk because once he moved toward me, I hit at him and I went outside so fast that I fell over the doorsill and sprawled in the dirt outside. We tried to push Walt inside to try to poke him out of hiding with the broom and Dave said "What are you, man or mouse?" Walt made the very fitting reply of "Give me a piece of cheese and I'll show you!" At any rate when the music started the tarantula came out. A sound movie of that would be precious! A phonograph blaring out a rumba and me jumping around swinging a broom as well as I could in a five foot. x five-foot room with Dave and Walt looking in the door! At long last I hit him and killed him, so now our troubles are over except for wondering if he has any friends. You know how every ship, plane etc. has a scoreboard of the planes etc. shot down-well this morning we painted a white tarantula on the side of the shack under "NOB Inc."

Just yesterday the radio said that discharge points had been lowered to 55 and here our 55 points left over a week ago. I just hope they keep up the good work.

On the "no smoking" deal. I went back to the pipe after a week. I just wanted to see if I could- and I could.

I used to think that when I get to the West Coast that I'd call you up before I did another thing. But now I don't think I will. I guess I will wire you, but the first thing I want to be able to do is kiss you and not just say hello and goodbye. If I called you it would make the train trip too long and unbearable.

Thurs., 12.6.1945, Saipan
A ship loaded with packages marked "Nauss" must have docked! I got three yesterday and three again today! And one is the second one from you. I didn't expect two! In a day or so I'll probably write to you that I've opened them. I have maintained they shouldn't be opened 'til Christmas, but all the other fellows are opening theirs as fast as they come in and I don't feel right about helping eat their stuff and leaving my packages unopened. Dave and I have packages under our beds, in our lockers, on the shelf, so today's batch decided us to build a food locker and pool our food.

When I just got to the island I wrote home for my old M.P. hat-the broad-brim job! Well, it came yesterday and already the whole area is agog. Everybody wants to know where I got it, how long I've been in the Army to rate one of those old hats, etc. Everybody wants to try it on and everybody-even the Gooks want to buy it. It's a swell hat 'tho and just the thing for rain and sun-I carry my own shade around. The bright gold and green case [?] attracts attention and one colored boy about wrecked his truck by turning around to look at me as I walked across the road.

The traffic is a thing to behold? About all the truck drivers now are Gooks or colored G.I.s and I don't know which is worse! Trucks race around; bump into each other, etc. Two days ago one colored Joe drove down to the docks too fast- couldn't stop and drove a 2 ½ ton truck right over the edge into 30 ft. of water! He got out OK, but it was just luck that he did!

Another group of new men came in today. They really aren't new to the Army 'tho most of them are fairly low point men. All the discharges drained their outfit so low that the outfit was dissolved and the rest of the men added to ours. Now we have a fairly good-sized outfit again, but they're all new faces and when you walk into a barrack you think you're in the wrong place.

Our 3 ½ year men are still all packed up ready to go. Rumor has it that they'll pull out next week. I sure hope that the next group takes all three-year men, but I'm "sweating it out" because they might decide to take married men or 3 ¼ years or something. If they do take all the three-year men at one time it'll be a big group of our outfit. This business of married men first, etc. and "Bring Daddy Home is a sore subject with us. After all, "all men are created equal" and since nobody asked them to get married why should they get home first. After all, if a man chooses to remain single all his life he has just as much right to be out of the Army as a man who chooses to marry.

Well, I'm a bad boy-I opened all my Christmas packages! When I got back from work Dave had the locker all set up and all stocked with the food and sweets of his loot, so I decided to open all mine and do the same.

I opened your first package Three rolls of film! No wonder you have trouble saving money-you spend it all on me. The nuts, cookies are a welcome addition to our party and I assure you I'll take good care of it. That "Rum Cake" business looks like you knew who you were sending it to. We have three Christmas trees on our shelf now and four (the family sent one) red candles. It even looks like Christmas! We have had some trouble getting tobacco we like and even then it's often moldy because it's just in cardboard packs. I said to Dave "Maybe she sent some Walnut" but no luck. I opened the family packages-candy, nuts, soap, shampoo, etc. and an aunt sent stationary and handkerchiefs. Then I opened your other package and lo and behold! A full pound of Walnut! And a glass jar to keep it fresh! I grinned at Bush and said "I knew my chick would come thru!"

You know my ring-the silver one? I broke it. It broke on the side about a week ago so I ran around and finally located some silver solder. I tried to fix it, but couldn't get an iron and torch that would work right. I was afraid it would come off so I kept it in my pocket rather than wear it I forgot and sent the jacket to the laundry with the ring in the pocket. One day after that I remembered it and by luck the laundry hadn't left the supply room yet, so I got it back and decided to wear it. Yesterday the other side broke and again I almost lost it! This time I wrapped it with Bud's silver bell and I'll leave it that way (with the camera lenses, shade and filter in the little square leather box you made) until I get home. So now I don't wear the ring, and I quit wearing Bud's bell when we got here and quit wearing the dog tags. But I still have the bracelet and it's in very good condition and "Love from Mer" means more to me every day.

Fri., 12.7.1945, Saipan
A Jap Captain and 60 of his men in the hills surrendered. They had been in hiding for 17 mos. in the hills. Supposedly there are still 10-150 in the hills (part of the 800 when the island was secured).

Men with 3 ½ years' service are leaving this week. I will be able to leave in the next batch with three years' service if they drop it to that.

Mon., 12.10.1945, Saipan
I feel like I'm in the middle of the dust bowl. There has been only a little rain and lots of sun in the past few days and now the wind is blowing clouds of dust around. The wind is unusual for this rock, because usually we have a dead cabin.

As far as we can learn, when we hit the West Coast we'll be put on troop trains and go right to our separation center (Meade I guess). In that case I guess it would be best for both of us if I waited those two days at Meade and didn't even try to see you until I was a newborn civilian and then we wouldn't have to part again for me to go back to Meade. I'm all in favor of meeting you first alone without telling anyone else I'm home. When I reach Calif. I'll wire you and the family that I'm safe in the States and will be home in several days. Then I'll call you from Meade and let you know when and where I'll get to Balto. [Baltimore] and you can meet me. How does that sound? I guess detailed plans like this are a bit premature since it'll probably be easily a month before I even leave the island, but after all our coming home is all we think about now.

So you think I should wear a shirt for my picture- just for our grandchildren. That's why we don't like this "Bring Daddy Home" rot. After all they already have their children and how will we single men ever have children, much less grandchildren, unless they let us come home? Well, as usual, I'm a wee bit ahead of you. Last week I got hold of a portrait attachment and had Dave try to take a few color shots of me. I even dug out a suntan shirt-smoothed it out- it's been packed in my duffle bag ever since we left the States-and pinned on our shoulder patch. But I doubt the pictures will be any good because the sun was very, very bright and as a result I'll probably have a Gawd awful look on my face. (I may have needed a shave too.)

Just had a letter from my brother. It seems he's been collecting stuff and now has a new Jap revolver and holster, a real samurai saber that is in good condition and "old enough to be a valuable antique" "also two short swords" and a number of blades of famous old swords makers 300 to 500 years old." He wrote me to ask if the Air Corps on Saipan is still paying fabulous prices for such stuff and if so he'd send or "fly them to me" and split the price with me. However, I'm afraid he's out of luck here since the Air Corps left bag and baggage last month and people not drawing flying pay don't pay prices like the $100 he says the sword is worth. He also says if he ever gets a chance to fly over here he'll bring some liquor as officers can get it but not sell it and I, as a G.I., could sell it but can't get it. The price here is between $25.00 and $35.00 per fifth! I think it's just a pipe dream 'tho that he could get a plane hop to Saipan because air traffic has dropped off a great deal in about the last month.

Wed., 12.12.1945, Saipan
We don't wear shorts or socks and we sleep on canvas cots.

Fri., 12.14.1945, Saipan
I miss you more than usual today and I know it'll be the same Christmas and New Year's. This Christmas I won't even have a friend of my girl's to tell my woes to. Somehow it doesn't seem possible that Christmas is only ten days away. The fourth of July would be more fitting to the season here.

Sun., 12.16.1945, Saipan
We haven't been on this rock a full three months yet and still it seems we must have been here at least six or eight months.

You should hear the radio now! They're playing recordings, but they announce "And now we bring you the music of Glen Gray playing at the new Gargan Beach Club on the island of Saipan" and the "Terrace Lounge of the Marzi Point County Club" . The way they announce it you'd almost think that such places really exist.

Maybe I can't go to Fords [Ford's Theatre, Washington, D.C.] like you and look at the new sconces but I did see a stage play the other night. Dave, another fellow and I drove up near Camp Savage to the "Turin Towers" to see "Kiss and Tell" put on by a U.S.O. troop that stopped here from Guam (everything, including our mail both ways goes thru Guam). Next they'll go to Okinawa, etc. It wasn't badly done and I've seen worse at Fords.

I don't know what stirred them up, but I got letters from two old flames yesterday. Lord but the latter seems like a flighty wench. I don't understand how I ever stood her. It looks like you don't have any worries darling. I'm trapped and I love it!

Maybe a lot of men have re-enlisted because they couldn't find apts., etc. but a lot are signing up again even before they get discharged. Going back to civilian life will be quite a change after several years of the Army and a lot of fellows are really afraid to go on their own again. But I still think they're nuts.

Mon., 12.17.1945, Saipan
Another drop tomorrow. 50-point men and men with 3½ years' service are leaving. That accounts for lots of fellows. I should be in the next drop and Bush
in the drop after that.

Tues., 12.18.1945, Saipan [Free postage postcard with picture of many people in swimming pool and Japanese writing.]
Feeling fine. The swimming is great. Wish you were here. Hope to see you soon.

Tues., 12.18.1945, Saipan
Only a week 'til Christmas and yet today is one of the hottest days we've had for weeks. It must easily be over ninety today.

I have news! Some of the 3 ½ year men left yesterday and the rest are leaving today. And note it's also reported that instead of staying at the casual depot for about a week that they'll be on the boat by tonight. Now in about a month the other islands should be able to clear their 3 ½ year men out and the ships can get back again. Then they should take the three-year boys! Walt and Dave each have
2½ years and they'll only be about a month behind me, but to hear them wish they were leaving when I do you'd think they were homesteading on Saipan. Our outfit is full of new faces now and there are only about twenty of us left that were together at Bowie. In a way we hate to see the boys go, but in lots more ways we're glad to see them go. I hope by the time I get there that Calif. won't be so crowded that we'll have to stay on the ship in the harbor like the news says they're doing now.

The second bit of news is about watches. Sat. there was a list to sign for men in the outfit who wanted to buy watches. I signed and told Dave to sign too since they draw names for them. Well it came out that they had 10 watches and my name wasn't drawn but Dave's was so I gave him the money, I picked out the watch, and he paid for it. Now I have a watch. It's a $24.00 "Felco"-Swiss-made, waterproof, shower proof, non-magnetic, sweep second hand and radium dial. I decided I wanted a watch without waiting 'til I got home and besides P.X. prices are at cost and much below retail in the States.

Remember the bracelet you gave me last Christmas? Yesterday if you had seen me pulling it apart you probably would have shot me first and asked questions afterward. Often I've wondered what I'd do with the bracelet after I became a civilian. I'd hate to quit wearing it because I like it and yet it would seem sort of foolish to wear an identification bracelet when there's no war or much chance that I'll need to be identified. I know lots of civilians do wear them, but I think a man's jewelry should serve a purpose. So, I took the bracelet apart and made it into a watchband. It's just the same as always only missing five links. I had thought about doing it before but the silver wouldn't match a gold watch, but the new watch is stainless steel. The six o'clock piece hooks on and off as a clasp. The bracelet plate is against the inside of my wrist. Now that they've seen it a lot of the fellows want to do the same things. These Nauss boys and their strange ideas!

The other day one of my Gooks gave me a packet of Japanese postcards. I mailed one to you this morning but don't ask me what the characters or pictures mean because I don't know and the Gooks don't know enough English to explain it to me.

We took the night off last night and went to see a movie. We had all seen it long ago but there was some horse opera at the other movie near us. As usual it rained thru half the show but we just sat with our ponchos on as usual. Among the many wonderful things about coming home will be to see a movie without getting rained on. But then, on the other hand, it might be hard to remember not to smoke during the show. Even the water will be a great thing. All our showering, shaving and washing is done with cold water.

P.S. The photo is just a trial but at least it shows wer're trying-shirt and all. I don't look that way all the time- the sun was bright. Maybe it's better he didn't show my hair-or lack of it.

Fri., 12.21.1945, Saipan
Saipan has gone "garrison". There are no more mixed uniforms, etc. We had felt that we were probably on the most relaxed island in the Pacific. I should be leaving in about three weeks. They are sending men back in groups according to where they live.

Tues., 12.25.1945, Saipan, Christmas Day
3:30 PM: Almost everybody here is sound asleep and I just got up myself. We had planned a dull Christmas Eve, but it turned out to be anything but that. Things started at 5:00 PM last evening when some early chowhounds reported that supper was fried Spam. About five of us had a fifth of rye that we were

dying to use, so we decided to make our Christmas Eve supper of fruitcake and rye. That gave us a nice start. Then we started to pool all our beer. We had big metal drums filled with cracked ice and our cold beer. About six fruitcakes spread out and about a 50 lb. burlap bag of mixed nuts. Somebody dragged in a large eight-foot pine tree, we lit the red candles, put the little trees around, and hung up white wool socks filled with nuts, etc. and a candy can sticking out the tops. Almost all of this was between Dave's and my beds, so that's where everyone gathered. Then for hours we proceeded to drink beer and sing. I put in one case of beer and altogether we must have had eight or ten cases! We sang everything that we knew and most of them several times. We were feeling no pain and at about 10:30 everyone had had enough and we ran out of beer at just the right time. We were just sinking into our sacks, tired but fairly happy and Bush went haywire. He was in a gay mood and the big sack of nuts was beside him. All of a sudden he started to throw nuts! He didn't just throw a few- he threw handfuls into the air like a rich miser gone mad. Nuts were going everywhere-it was raining nuts. We were all laughing so hard we could hardly move, but finally I got the bag away from him and we all went to bed. It was a gay party, but what a mess in the morning! The place was almost knee-deep in beer bottles, nuts, bottle caps, the ice had all melted and run over so there was water all over the floor-there were nuts in our beds, in our clothes, in our shoes. We cleaned the place up, but we're still finding nuts everywhere. Bush is really taking a kidding about that today! Needless to say, we didn't get up for breakfast. Dinner was 12:00 so we slept, loafed, and had bull-sessions 'til then. Oh yes, one fellow broke out a 1fifth of brandy so we took care of that as the "hair of the dog that bit us".

Dinner was fine-just like Thanksgiving. Then each man was also given a carton of cigarettes, pipe tobacco, soap, toothbrush, etc.

Thurs., 12.27.1945, Saipan
Bush and I finally got an extra footlocker and put it between our beds and put all or food together. We have cheese, popcorn, nuts, candy, cookies, and fruit. Bush also has tobacco, two decks of cards, five rolls of film and two small Christmas trees. I have

two smaller trees and two red candles. We took photographs on Christmas morning. I took one of Bush with his tree and presents and he took one of me but cut my head off.

Fri., 12.28.1945, Saipan
Well, the day's work is almost done. The Gooks are changing clothes to go home and my night man will be here soon to take them to Susupe. Then when he gets back I can leave for the day. The Gooks and I have both had a hard day. I managed to borrow another air compressor so we managed to cut down on the Christmas rush backlog so that we only have about 60 tires to be aired up and then we'll be all caught up-just in time to fall behind on New Year's. Well, at least we've never fallen behind to the point where we didn't have a tire already to go for every flat that came in.

Tomorrow we turn in most of our field equipment and extra clothes that we won't bring home. That's just one more step towards coming home and it means they expect us to leave at least within two weeks. When I get home I'll have to sit down and just say over and over again "I am home! I am home!" I can plan on tomorrow and next week and next year and five years from now.

I've changed my mind and I will bring that Patent Off. application home instead of sending it ahead. The ideas is that I've run into a bit of trouble on home and business addresses of former employers and ref. and there's no phone book here to look it up. Then to, I should check on the exact designation of my civil service rating, etc.

Sun., 12.30.1946, Saipan
We're still talking about going home, but that's all we're doing-talking. Two carriers are out in the harbor now and we're hoping that we'll ride one of them back. Rumors are still flying but nothing is sure. We've been encouraged by letters that several of our boys have been flown from the West to the East Coast.

What's all this business of having silver made? You know a lot more about those things than I, but it seems to me that the price would be way above that of a stock pattern. Then too, with a pattern that is in stock you could almost count on getting some wedding gifts that would match. But then I notice that you say "continue" with an outmoded pattern. So, I guess a great deal depends on how much you have of that pattern.

Now you have all the pictures, both color and black and white. That is if the last batch of slides have reached you from Eastman and they should have by now. We seem to have just about exhausted the rock of picture possibilities. Now the only ones I want to take are the ones to record the trip home to you.

We killed today just by sleeping and loafing in general. It has been cloudy and raining off and on all day long so it wasn't worthwhile to swim or even wash clothes. But tomorrow I'll have to do some washing rain or shine. We're afraid to send laundry because we may be sent up to the casual depot any day and we want to be all set to go.

Tues., 1.1.1946, Saipan
Gee, I started this letter last year and I'm just getting back to it. Here I've had 3 ½ days off from work and I haven't even finished one letter. Everybody else is in the same fix and we just can't see how the time goes so fast and we got so little done.

At least I did get my laundry finished and what a job. Our method is to spread the things out on a piece of plywood and scrub the h--- out of them with a heavy brush. It isn't so good on the clothes, but it does the job fairly well even in spite of cold water. I also got a great white wash. Our methods usually end up with yellows and tattletale grey-but I tried something I heard about and it worked swell. I dumped half a bottle of Halazone tablets into the water. They made a wonderful bleach and since we were all issued four or five bottles and we don't need to treat our drinking water, so we may as well use them for something.

Last night we had a beer party to see the old year out. At midnight we stood outside and watched the ships in the harbor. Searchlights were fanning back and forth across the sky, guns were being fired and red, green and white flares were being shot in the air. It reminded me of a Fourth of July bombardment of Fort McHenry [Baltimore, MD] only on a large scale.

This morning we all had more or less of a hangover and it was raining outside so we slept thru breakfast. Then we rolled over and ate cheese and crackers, nuts, coffee and fruit juice without even getting out of bed. Yes, we even made coffee with my little stove and K ration coffee without getting out of bed! We find that four times the advised amount of coffee makes it as strong as we like. Then we gradually got into a battle of throwing nuts. I got the worst of it since my bunk is nearly in the center so they all ganged up on me. When I got tired of being hit I crawled under the blanket-then they did gang up on me. The first thing I knew my cot was turned upside down with me still in it. What a way to play when you have a hangover! After being rolled on the floor I needed a shower. That cured the hangover! It was raining hard and the water hadn't been warmed by the sun, so it was ice cold.

Here's something we just learned about today: About a month ago a Jap captain gave himself up with 40 of his men. They had been hiding in the woods for a year. For the past few weeks he has been getting other groups of Japs to give themselves up. Now we learn that he is missing- he had gone into the hills to locate some Japs and he just didn't come back. Now we're all wondering if the Japs still on the loose shot him for quitting or if he just found a good way to turn over the men who wanted to quit and then gave us the slip.

Sat., 1.5.1946, Saipan
I don't know where all my letters have been going or how they could have been delayed so much. I've written a lot more than you seem to have received. I haven't been sick. I haven't had an accident, nothing has upset me. I haven't been working hard. I haven't even <u>seen</u> another tarantula.

We had a nice swim for the first time in about two weeks. By we I mean five of us, a rubber life raft and half a case of beer. We drove over to Kagman Point where there is a good place in

Magicienne Bay. You can dive off the 15 ft. cliff into the ocean. The water is between 30-40 feet deep. The water is so clear you can see right to the bottom. Besides we had a diving mask that fits over your eyes and nose so we could swim underwater and look at the strange fish and rocks. There were all sizes and shapes of fish and all colors of the rainbow. I'll swear I saw one that looked like he was wearing a yellow and blue sports jacket!

We had to climb down a 15 ft. iron ladder and step onto a four-foot rubber boat that is bouncing on the surf. The boat couldn't stay close to shore more than a moment because if a wave dashed it against that coral cliff--- I decided one slip and my camera would be junk We rowed as close under the cliff as we could and the fellow on the land threw the bottle opener into the boat. Patton was in the bow and he tried to catch the first beer and it went right thru his hands. (The bottle was wet.) Bush had the diving mask on so he went down for it and brought it up from 30 ft. where it was bouncing around on the rocks. While he was after that we caught the 2nd and 3rd bottles. The fourth we missed, but yours truly was overboard right after it and caught it halfway down. Then we all lay in the boat and drank beer much to the envy of those on the cliff. After that we rowed to the cliff again and were thrown cigarettes and matches!

We've just got back and heard the news broadcast about an idea to slow up discharges and keep men 30-40 days after they are ready for discharge. Also, we heard that we may not move up to the casual depot 'til the 15th.

The family will know when I reach the States but I'll call you first when I get to Meade.

Mon., 1.7.1946, Saipan
I've moved around a lot in the Army but I've never sweated out every last minute like this before. At least most people seem sure that this slowdown of discharge won't affect us.

And another crisis! They just told us this noon that the Koreans won't be back to work in the morning or after that. This is their last day. And now they tell us! Tomorrow they'll send down three men (G.I.'s) from each company. They'll have to do the work of repairing the tires. It's going to be a headache and a screwed up mess and I thank the Lord that I won't have to put up with it for more than a day or two. They're going to send down a 3-year man. Why not put someone in that they won't to have replace in one or two days? I wonder how dumb you have to be to be a Lt.?

You should see the form letter that's being passed around here about how demobilization is being screwed up. Thousands were passed out and still we've only been able to get one each. After all they told us we're fighting a war for what was right and now we have to fight the peace for what we think is right.

Wed., 1.9.1946, Saipan
What a mail system! I've had about one letter in the past week, and then today at noon I got <u>eight</u> and this evening two more and a package! The package was tobacco that the family forgot to send at Christmas and sent by first class mail. All the letters were 3-cent jobs and they must have made the trip by boat this time. The dates ranged from Nov. 30th (39 days!) to Dec. 11th.

There's another fellow in our outfit now from Balto.[Baltimore] so I can pass the newspapers along to him. He also has three yrs. service so we can expect to go from here to Meade together… if, as, and when.

The jingles your dad [Edward Alford Stabler] sent arrived too and we got a kick out of them- and we can use laughs now because our morale is at an all-time low.
Night before last the brand new laundry burned down. They were building it ever since we hit this rock and it was only finished two weeks ago. It was the largest building on the rock and all wood. The laundry that went in last Sat. was the first to be done in the new building and darned if it didn't burn to the ground and all the clothes with it! Besides that we were to start paying $1.50 per month for laundry- it had been free before! The damage is valued at one million dollars and there's a lot of question as to how it started. Just by Nauss luck I didn't send any in to be done thinking we'd be leaving soon, so it wasn't

safe not to be ready. The G.I. clothing will be replaced, but not "T shirts", etc.

You ask if we don't have days in the tire shop when "everything works in apple-pie order?" No! no, no, a thousand times no! I never thought our tire days would come to this. Our Gooks went away on the truck the day before yesterday. For at least the past week I had been telling them that "bossman go home any day now." Then as the Gooks drove away they said goodbye-waved and yelled: "Bossman no go home?" That hurt. Here I told them I was going home and they leave before I do! Maybe we were in the wrong army! They sent us two men from each company in the battalion-12 men and 10 men from the Navy. Then they provided me one of our Sgts. As a boss of the labor gang. I'm still in charge of the shop so that I have to tell the Sgt. (good friend of mine) what should be done and how and he gets the men to do it. But it doesn't work. The Gooks had been on that job for a long time and knew just what to do and how to do it; and they worked hard. These men are new, and not too eager. In all the time we had the Gooks they never went home one evening that there was an unrepaired tire in the place. Yesterday after our first day with G.I.'s there were 40 flats left unrepaired. The officers are too bull-headed to listen to us or realize that 22 new G.I.'s can't do the work of 38 experienced Gooks- and they won't realize it until we run out of tires and they have to pull trucks off the road. A driver would take better care of his tires if he had to fix them himself.

I guess you've seen plenty in the papers about the protests, letters, wires, etc. of men overseas who think the discharges aren't going as fast as possible. It's the same way here and we're all mad as hell. Protest letters are being printed by the thousands and we're all sending them to our Senators, etc. I sent one today to *The Sun* [Baltimore newspaper]. Even our newspaper here *The Target* today published a list of all senators so every G.I will know who to address his letters. It's rumored that this "slowdown" won't bother the 3-year men and that Saipan isn't included in it because it isn't considered a hostile zone; but here we are. There's a carrier waiting to take us home and the casual depot is waiting to process us (They can handle 3,000 men and only have 400 up there now.) the only reason we're not aboard the ship is that they're awaiting the orders about this "discharge slowdown" to be cleared up.

Thurs., 1.10.1946, Saipan "The Rock"
Bud and lots of others heard on the radio today that Gen. "Ike" told all area commanders to send their men home as soon as possible. I hope with all my heart that they don't change their minds and decide to make it 3 ¼ years because the date for 3-years service was set at Feb. 1st and I'd miss 3 ¼ yrs. by 24 days.

The tire shop, that place is still losing ground and now there are 99 tires not repaired (Tues.-40, Wed.-63, Thurs.-99).

We know that about two weeks ago a bag of mail fell out of a cargo net and is at the bottom of the ocean now. It was outgoing mail and even most of the airmail goes by boat to Guam first.

Fri., 1.11.1946, Saipan
Maybe Doris Mindas (sp?) feels the same way about me since I haven't written her cards or anything, but I didn't realize that she and Geo. were engaged I didn't know (and I don't know that the family did either) until he mentioned in a letter that she wanted to get married soon after he returned.

Sat., 1.12.1946, Saipan
Honey, when you read this I'll be on my way home to you! I'm up at the casual depot now. I don't hope to go, I'm there! At noon today we heard that the official drop would be to 48 points or 38 months service. I just got under the 38 months with seven days to spare. It was a blow to most of the fellows as most of them just had three years and now they'll have to wait 'til next month.

At noon after we heard the news we said "Well, we'll probably go to casual Tues. or Wed." We went on with our plans to swim like last Sat. We loaded the beer and rubber boats into the truck and got in. Just as we were starting the motor someone poked his head in and said "Nauss and McHenry- be ready to leave at 3:00 PM!" It was 1:30 PM then! It started to rain anyway, so we sat around and drank the beer while two of us threw our stuff in a bag. It rained and we got soaked but nothing in the world could make us mad. We got to casual at 5:30 PM and had a makeshift supper of cold Spam, cold corn, and cold peas, but we were happy. We filled out a lot of forms and now we're in our tent for the night. Tomorrow will be more processing and baggage inspection. Our ship expects to leave Monday night or Tuesday AM. We're going on a big job- the aircraft carrier *Hornet.* With good weather the *Hornet* should make it in 15 days or so and I should wire you from the West Coast not long after the 30th. This may be the last letter until I wire.

I love you so very much dear and I'm on my way home to you.

Tues., 1.15.1946 APO 244 c/o P.M. San Francisco, Calif., from Saipan (but not for long)
We are finished with processing except for customs declarations of our bags. Three quarters of the fellows finished yesterday but not me. We were supposed to sail on the *Hornet* but it was sent to Guam instead. We'll go on a medium carrier, the *Independence* leaving tomorrow. We should get to the States around the end of next month and that's better time than the *Julian* made. I'm sure I'm coming to Meade for my discharge.

Sat., 1.26.1946 [Western Union telegram]
Meade shipment left me behind. Lots of love. Allen

Sat., 1.26.1946, Saipan
We had an unexpected drop this afternoon and several others and I got left behind. Our bunch is leaving with 48 points or 38 month's service.

Sun**., 1.27.1946, Saipan**
This business of the discharges being slowed down may bring down so much public opinion on the Army that they may go on at the usual rate. And then too it may only apply to hostile zones where replacements are needed.

I hope they move us up to the casual depot tomorrow or at least Tues. and don't put it off. In the *Target* newspaper today the headline was "You're Stuck!"

CHAPTER 8
Coming Home

Tues., 1.29.1946 [Western Union telegram]
Landed today flying East will call from Meade about Fri. All my love Allen

Fri., 2.1.1946
Bush left. To be discharged from Fort MacArthur [Los Angeles, CA]. He should be home around Feb.20th.

[Undated note]
Just a word or two about your bit of Plexiglas. It started out by being built as a B-26 Bomber built by Martin in Baltimore (funny it starts and ends in Baltimore). I don't know just where the plane went from there, but somewhere along the line it picked up the name "Scalded Dog" and bombed Germany. These bits of glass are from the center panel of the nose or the "bomb window" so the bombsight looked thru your earrings over Germany for 50 missions (only they weren't your earrings then). After 50 missions the "Scalded Dog" was retired and sent back to the U.S. for training. Then it cracked up here and I figured your trinket may as well have a history instead of being made of new and inexpensive plexi. I'm afraid they are a bit larger than they should be for earrings, but I didn't realize that 'til too late and besides it was still small enough to make 'tho hard to work with. The imperfect workmanship assures that they are handmade. Nothing will ever match the stars in your eyes, but you said you'd like a bit of plexi.

Thurs., undated note, St. Louis station [on USO letterhead]
Have a bit of a layover here but still on my way. Arrived in Pitt. [?] As fresh and clean as if I had mined coal all day. Leg from Pitt. to St. L. [St. Louis, MO] was not nearly so bad and here to Fort Worth should be OK. Got here right on time, but I sure made an error on the train from here to Fort

W. I'll have a five-hour stop here instead of the three as I had expected. However, it will be a faster train than I figured on so I'll get to Fort W. even earlier than I had requested and have plenty of time.
According to one trainman the stretch between Balto. and Pitt. is so dirty because they usually oil the roadbed every year and this year they don't have the oil.

Have spent the past two hours washing up, shaving, and getting breakfast here in the station. We'll take a short look at the town if it isn't raining too hard.

I wonder how long I'll have to be away from you this time before the sharp heartache of parting settles down to the dull lasting ache of being away from you?

My father and mother were at the station when I left, but it was like meeting them along the way since I really left when I walked out of your office.

I love you very much darling, and I'll never be really happy until we are together to stay.

Chapter 9
The Rest of the Story

How They Met

Young people generally hung around in groups to socialize more so than as dating couples. Allen and Mercia had been in some of the same social settings such as going swimming, dancing, and to parties. Eleanor Stratton and Mercia were friends. Eleanor was dating Allen and Mercia was dating someone else when they went on a double-date to dinner at the Anchorage Restaurant in Annapolis overlooking the U.S. Naval Academy on the Severn River. Eleanor wanted to talk to Mercia's date so she sent Allen to keep Mercia company. They watched a man try to throw his wife over the railing at the restaurant. Eleanor was subsequently her maid/matron of honor at their wedding.

Her Parent's Version of Allen and Mercia's Engagement

Allen telephoned Mercia's father to say they were going to go out to dinner after the Duke-Navy football game at the Baltimore Stadium on October 14, 1944. Her father asked Allen what the score was of the game and Allen couldn't remember. When the conversation ended, her father turned to his wife and told her that something was up!

The Final Chapter

After Allen's discharge from the U.S. Army in February 1946, he married Mercia Evelyn Stabler on May 25, 1946 in Baltimore. They lived in a small apartment near Baltimore's Washington monument while he obtained his law degree at night school from the University of Baltimore. [I'm not aware that he ever took the bar exam.]

Allen went to work as a purchasing agent for the Black and Decker Company in Parkton, MD. In 1949, Allen and Mercia moved to Glen Rock, PA. Their first child, Christine, was born in 1950. Their son, Allen Howard Nauss, Jr., was born in 1955. Around 1957, Allen took a job as purchasing agent for the Hardinge Manufacturing Company and the family moved to York, PA He worked there until he retired in 1983. Several months later he and Mercia had gone to dinner with Eleanor Stratton Bacon and her husband Charles. He fell unconscious driving home and died three days later from a brain aneurysm.

Allen & Mercia's wedding day, May 25, 1946

APPENDIX I

Allen H. Nauss- Timeline

1/4/1919	Born at West End Mt. Hospital, Baltimore, MD
1933-1937	Attended and graduated from Forest Park High School, Baltimore, MD
Unknown	Formerly with "Phila. Ordnance Dist." "Balto. Sub. Off.", other reference as civilian ordnance inspector; 10/30/1945 mentioned still had Civil Service rating since he was on furlough from Ordnance
9/1937-6/1939	Two years of basic infantry ROTC in 4th Brigade while attending University of Maryland, College Park, MD (Mechanical Engineering major)
1938	Welder's Assistant, Crown, Cork & Seal Company, Baltimore, MD and Inspector of sheet steel at Bethlehem Steel Company, Sparrows Point, Baltimore, MD
1940-1942	Attended but did not graduate from night school as law student, at University of Baltimore, Baltimore, MD. Also studied French
3/17/1941	Staff clerk during day and law clerk compiling statistics (5 mos.) in evenings for Baltimore Criminal Justice Commission, Inc. when inducted
12/1941-4/1942	Basic training, U.S. Army Air Forces, Seymour Johnson Field, Goldsboro, NC (base opened
9/1942	Inspector, Ordnance Mtls., War Dept., Philadelphia Ordnance Dist., Baltimore Office for three branches of Revers, Copper & Brass Works, Baltimore, MD
9/14/1942	Applied for enlistment in Air Forces Enlisted reserve as ground crew
>10/5/1942	Served with Co. I, 1302 S.O. Camp George G. Meade, MD
11/17 /1942	Inducted into Army, Local Board #23, Baltimore, MD
11/24/1942	Entry into Active Service (Baltimore) and reported to Ft. George G. Meade, Maryland

12/22/1942- Stationed with HQ o. C, 703rd MP Bn Air Corps assigned to 1350th S.U. (SCAA CD), Ft. Myer, VA

12/1942-2/1943 Co. C, 703 M.P. Bn (2I)

2/19/1943 Became a PFC

2/27/1943 Left HQ Mil. Dist. of Washington, D.C.

2/27/1943-4/10/1943 8th Prov. Ord. Tng. Co.

1943 Basic training at Ft. Myer, VA, classified as Infantry Rifleman

2/27/1943-? Attended 8th Ordnance Training Company School, Aberdeen Proving Grounds, Maryland-hand & shoulder weapons

4/10/1943 (S.A. 101)-6 week course in repair of small arms weapons

4/14/1943 Qualified for aviation cadet appointment

4/21/1943 Physical examination performed at Bolling AFB, Washington, D.C.

Bef.4/25/1943 Stationed at Pentagon, Washington, D.C. (formerly an M.P., traffic control, possibly at the Pentagon and later at Lake Charles, LA)

1943 Possibly trained with 3rd U.S. Infantry at Ft. Myer in Arlington, VA

9/-/1943 Stationed at Seymour Johnson Field

9/4/1943 Became PFC for second time

9/6-12/1943- 722 Tng. Det. Aun. Cadet Non-Fly, Seymour Johnson Field, Goldsboro, NC

10/1/1943 Elected to TRN as A/G GND CREW

12/30/1943- Attended Yale University for AFTS 3/24/44 training, New Haven, CT, five-week course in aircraft armament repair

1/1944-3/1944 Aviation cadet, 999th Air Corps Tech. School, New Haven, CT

1/6/1944- Washed out of armament course on

2/25/1944 -failed Engineering Physics

3/24/1944 Stationed at Lake Charles, LA

10/1/1944 BU CCTS CAAF BLK, Lake Charles, LA

10/14/1944 Became engaged

7/44-11/1944 Lake Charles, LA

1944 Visit or stationed in Princeton, NJ

12/1944	Reference to formerly at Lake Charles, LA as armourer at Army Air Base
12/1944	Letter thanked him for his Air Corps service
12/1944	Will get second classification as Infantry Rifleman
12/1944	Now in his "5th branch of the service within two years" Commented that he hasn't been in the Navy yet
12/11/1944	With Hq IARTC-Cp, Camp Maxey, TX
12/9-14/1944	Had been at Camp Maxey, TX at least this long
12/9/1944	CG IARTC, Cp, Howze, TX
Undated	Believed to have gone from Lake Charles, LA to Camp Maxey, TX
1/26/1945	Ft. Meade shipment left him behind
1/28/45	Going to Camp Bowie from unknown location (Camp Maxey?) around 11/30 to a place 300-400 mi. south of current location. Has been stationed at Maxey, Houge, and then Bowie
2/26/1945	Friends thought he was in Germany
4/1945	Stationed with 470th QM Truck Co. Cp., Bowie, TX
4/16/1945	PFC. Western Chemical Warfare School, RMA, Denver, CO, four week course in handling poison gas
4/1945-5/1945	Attended Western Chemical Warfare Training School, Rocky Mountain Arsenal Denver, CO.
4/23/1945	Had been an armorer, gunner, gun instructor, assistant truck driver, chemical warfare instructor, and "metrologist"
5/1945	Has 30 "points", one for each month of service
6/10/1945	Reference to former weather at Camp Houge, TX
7/1945	Previously was in Lake Charles, LA
7/18/1945	Previously had been stationed at Ft. Myer, near Washington, D.C.
7/8/1945	Return address listed as PFC A.H. Nauss, 33384264, 470th Q.M., Camp Bowie
8/22-27/1945	Arrived in Ft. Lawton, Seattle, WA then to Ft. Lewis, WA for five days, then back to Ft. Lawton, WA

8/30/1945	Left Seattle, WA for Pearl Harbor, HI on the *U.S.S. George W. Julian*
9/16/1945	Arrived in Saipan (approx. 6,500 mi. from Seattle to HI to Atoll to Saipan); new APO address is 244 (Saipan). No longer in 4th Army (TX) and 2nd (TN)-they are only used stateside
9/25/1945	Arrived in Saipan
9/26/1945	Rumor says that they're under the First. Div. and under Pearl Harbor command.
10/16/1945	Made rank of Corporal (TEC 5)
11/24/1945	Left for Ft. Meade, MD
1/29/1945	Envelope: T/5, A.H. Nauss, 33384264, 470th Q.M. Trk Co., APO 244, c/o P.M., San Francisco, CALIF.
1/2/1946	Left Saipan and headed home with 170th Q.M. Truck Co.
1/29/1946	Landed in the U.S. and flying to the East Coast
2/2/1946	Honorably discharged separation from Army at Fort George G. Meade, MD

Assignments

3 ¼ months-PVT-Corps of Military Police Basic Training
7 months-PFC-Military Police
8 months-PFC armourer
9 months-TEC5 Foreman, Labor 356
Supervised 38 natives in breakdown, repair and assembling truck tires. Kept and filed timecards, reports, and correspondence. Requisitioned necessary supplies and equipment.

Decorations/Citations/Awards

MKM Pistol Carbine SS Rifle N-1
Good Conduct Medal
Asiatic Pacific Theater Ribbon
American Theater Ribbon
World War II Victory Ribbon

Appendix I

APPENDIX II

Updates on Service Buddies

David "Dave" M. Bush was born 3 Nov 1924, formerly lived in Monterey, CA, and died Sept. 2011 in Carmel, CA. His wife, Virginia, died 22 Feb. 2013. They had children George Bush (Alvita), Connie Stoaks (Jim), and Margo Fuselier (Donald).

Walter "Walt" O'Connell was originally from Denver, CO. He was born 28 Sept 1924. He married Doris Hicks in 1945 and they had two daughters. His wife died in 1949. Walt married Fern Steelsmith in 1952. He was employed by the State of Colorado for 30 years. He was a musician and played with several local dance bands as a drummer and a vocalist. He was a member of the Masonic Lodge and Fern was a member of the Order of Eastern Star. His greatest wish was to see the WWII memorial in Washington, D.C. He was a charter member of that memorial. In July, 2008 he traveled to see it with the Rocky Mountain Honor Flight. Walt d. 9 Feb 2013 in Denver, CO. Fern died 23 Nov 2013. Both are buried at Ft. Logan National Cemetery. They had daughters, Cathie Newton (Dennis) and Sandra Tekavec (Dan)

Clyde B. Helzer was born 17 June 1920 and was from Nebraska His wife was Kathleen Hughes. Clyde died 28 July 1997 in Fort Worth, TX. His wife died 13 Sept 2008 in Ft. Worth, TX. They had no known children.

Updates on Friends

Charles August Rausch, Jr., was born 28 Mar 1919 and died 11 Oct 2011. He was married to Josephine "Betty" Sandlas Rausch and was best man at Allen's wedding

Louis "Lou" M. Hatter was born 18 Aug 1919 and died 21 Apr 1988.

"Bud" Henderson was born 15 Mar ___. He married to Jane ____ on Mar. 17, 1945. No additional information was found.

Josephine "Jo" Henry Cox was born 1 May 1920 and died 25 July 2004. She was a former Girl Scout Leader and never married.

Eleanor Stratton Bacon, b. 8 July 1922 in Baltimore, d., 11 May 2012. Spouse: Charles W. Bacon. They had children Stephen, Brian

INDEX

About the Editor

Christine N. Simmons

Christine "Tina" N. Simmons had an interest in genealogy from a very early age. She first tried to research her father's military history a number of years ago but was told, like many others, that his military records had been burned in the St. Louis, Missouri fire. Several years later she repeated the process and was surprised to receive a large stack of copies of slightly burned records including a trove of information about where and when her father had been stationed.

Tina's family includes a grown son, Michael Samuel Simmons, and grown grandson, Cody Michael Petenbrink, younger brother, Allen Howard Nauss, Jr. twin nephews, Allen John "A.J." Nauss and Jonathan Michael "Jon" Nauss. A.J. is a career Navy man and Jon enlisted in the Army and went through Officer's Training School.

Tina currently makes her home in Laurel, Maryland where she lives with her long-time companion, Dennis.